The
TRUTH
ABOUT
Women

The
TRUTH
ABOUT
Women

Fighting the

Fourteen Devastating

Myths That Hold

Women Back

Dr. Georgia Witkin

VIKING

VIKING
Published by the Penguin Group
Penguin Books USA Inc., 375 Hudson Street,
New York, New York 10014, U.S.A.
Penguin Books Ltd, 27 Wrights Lane,
London W8 5TZ, England
Penguin Books Australia Ltd, Ringwood,
Victoria, Australia
Penguin Books Canada Ltd, 10 Alcorn Avenue,
Toronto, Ontario, Canada M4V 3B2
Penguin Books (N.Z.) Ltd, 182–190 Wairau Road,
Auckland 10, New Zealand

Penguin Books Ltd, Registered Offices:
Harmondsworth, Middlesex, England

First published in 1995 by Viking Penguin,
a division of Penguin Books USA Inc.

10 9 8 7 6 5 4 3 2 1

Results from poll appearing on Prodigy service January 13–
February 3, 1995, used by permission of Prodigy Services Co.
Copyright © 1995 Prodigy Services Co. All rights reserved.

LIBRARY OF CONGRESS CATALOGING-IN-PUBLICATION DATA
Witkin, Georgia.
The truth about women / Georgia Witkin.
    p.   cm.
ISBN 0-670-85060-8
1. Women—United States.   2. Women—United States—Public
opinion.   3. Stereotype (Psychology)—United States.
4. Sexism—United States.   I. Title.
HQ1421.W57   1995
305.4′0973—dc20   95-20345

This book is printed on acid-free paper.

Printed in the United States of America
Set in Bodoni Book
Designed by Kathryn Parise

ACKNOWLEDGMENTS

Let me tell you the truth about Mindy Werner.

She cheered and pushed and shaped and compiled and composed and corrected and cross-checked and assisted and comforted and commiserated and sustained this book and this author. She has been dedicated to *The Truth About Women*. *The Truth About Women* is now dedicated to her!

Let me also acknowledge the many others who contributed so much. My thanks . . .

To Joan Lippert Indig, for her devotion to this project, organizational talents, recommendations, and revisions. She encouraged my research about women when she was my editor at *Health* magazine, and continues a decade later as my friend.

To my colleagues at Mt. Sinai School of Medicine in New York City, for the support they've given my research and for their willingness to share their research: Dr. Richard Berkowitz, Dr. Kenneth Davis, Dr. Gary Rosenberg, Dr. Alexis Karstaedt, Dr. Philip Luloff, Dr. Raul Schiavi, Dr. Hillel Swiller, Dr. Maria Bustillo, Dr. Larry Grunfeld, Dr. Benjamin Sandler, Irma Damhuis, and Mel Granick.

To Dr. Leonard Lustgarten, Dr. Barry Weintraub, Dr. Rob Reiner, Dr. Gordon Ball, Katie Hardy, and Deserie Osborne, for their fact-checking and interest.

To WNBC, for tremendous institutional support, and to my associates at WNBC, who cheered on this project: Bill Bolster, Bruno Cohen, Dan Forman, Kim Gerbasi, Grant Winter, Donovan Myrie, Terry Doll,

Carl Killingsworth, Gloria Clyne, and particularly Dave Browde, who made the PRODIGY poll a reality, and Ramona Schindelheim, who read the manuscript with a television producer's eye.

To Kate Deane Robinson and the team at PRODIGY, for their cooperation and enthusiasm.

To Don Epstein, Cara Epstein, Kenny Rahtz, and Barbara Solomon at Greater Talent Network, and to Grada Fisher, Dee-Ann Mernit, and Iris Kessler at Fisher Ross Associates, and to Susan Smirnoff and Susan Lichtendorf at Ruder-Finn, for making the local polls possible.

To Michael Braverman, for his scholarly contributions and conversations.

To Lenore Skenazy, *Daily News* columnist and humorist extraordinaire, for her take on the media's portrait of women.

And of course to the women in my life who teach me the "truth about women" every day: My dear friend (my daughter's godmother), Connie Freeman; my wonderful assistant (or is it the other way around?), Roberta Gallagher; my teammate (and moral support) at Mt. Sinai, Dr. Alexis Karstaedt; my favorite sister-in-law (mother of Nikki and Jenny), Laurie Witkin; my brilliant and generous mother, Dr. Mildred Witkin-Radovic; and my wise and loving daughter, Kimberly.

CONTENTS

PREFACE

The millennium is coming and it's time for the truth about women:

—We *don't* love men who hate us.

—We are *not* mechanical or mathematical imbeciles.

—We're *not* devastated by midlife or menopause or men.

—We're *not* trying to trap men into marriage (it increases their sense of life satisfaction more than it does ours).

—We're *not* more interested in sex as we age (we lose partners, not libido).

—We're *not* out of control when we're shopping (we buy groceries and kids' underwear; most big-ticket purchases like boats and recreational vehicles are bought by men).

—And we're *not* crazed when we're premenstrual (studies say that, hormonally, we just become more the way men are . . . all month long!).

It's time for the facts, because knowledge is power. Myths create confusion and self-fulfilling prophecies. Knowledge helps us understand our past and prepare for our future. Myths make us feel hopeless. Knowledge creates choices.

And more than any other group of women since the dawn of time, we are women used to choices—choices we can now offer to our daughters:

—We have technological choices our grandmothers never had, such as contact lenses, plastic surgery, birth control, and assisted reproductive technologies.

—We have new career choices like the fields of finance, computers, law enforcement, and the aerospace industry.

—And, of course, we have lifestyle choices:

- *We no longer experience empty-nest syndrome.* When the nest empties, we can redecorate or move more into the world ourselves.
- *We no longer suffer from midlife crises.* Menopause symptoms are now an inconvenience, not a tragedy.
- *We no longer use hormones just to control pregnancy.* We use them to get pregnant. (So some of us have morning sickness at forty-five, and some of us have hot flashes.)
- *We're not little girls looking for "big daddies" or "sugar daddies."* We are the self-sufficient women living through the "baby-boom" era, and 7 million "babies" will become middle-aged by 1996!

And although it's been popular to say women don't really want information and choices because we don't dare take the responsibility that goes with them, my research doesn't agree. Women report that the only time they say, "I don't care," to a choice is when the decision is trivial—such as, "What movie do you want to see?" or, "Where should we go for dinner?"—and the reason isn't low self-esteem, it's exhaustion. When decisions count, we make choices, we take choices, we are not afraid of choices. In fact, most women say they *need* a sense of choice to prevent stress.

We don't have the kind of self-esteem problem everyone seems to think we have, either. Survey after survey now finds that when our self-esteem does drop, it's more frequently the result, not the cause, of how we treat ourselves. And they also find that we are *not* dissatisfied with our bodies, our capacity to handle stress, or our appearance, either (although we tend to talk about self-improvement endlessly).

This unfortunately does not mean that sexism is dead. Young women still say there's a sexual double standard, and working women still hit a glass ceiling with unequal pay for equal (or superior) work. It's just that the consequence of this sexism isn't always female self-blame or low self-esteem. To tell women it is adds insult to injury.

If you're wondering why there are so many myths about women . . . so much psychobabble, there are many reasons:

↦ *Myths are dramatic.* Whenever we call a woman the boss from hell or a bad driver or "Mommie Dearest," there's always a story attached. What we forget is that even if the story is true, it's just one story. There are plenty of male bosses from hell, bad men drivers, and "Daddy Dearests," too.

   ↔ ***Myths are "convenient."*** Social psychologists tell us that categorizing is an innate information-processing ability that helps us interact quickly and easily with hundreds of people a week. But when categorizing becomes stereotyping, it gets in the way of personal interaction and perpetuates myths.

   ↔ ***Myths are camouflage.*** Even though many men and women are not threatened by a woman who makes more money, runs faster, or knows more about cars, some are, and we may be tempted to allow them to use the myths of female powerlessness or incompetence to ease tension when we are dealing with such people.

The price of these myths, however, is too high. Competent and powerful women inadvertently undermine themselves and other women; daughters learn misinformation from mothers, men, or the media; young women begin to feel hopeless, inadequate, or estranged; and communication, trust, and even love between men and women becomes more difficult.

But I'm here to tell you that women seem ready to give up the myths and learn the truth. A Roper poll finds most women are annoyed by jokes about women drivers, mothers-in-law, or dumb blondes. A Parke-Davis company poll I designed two years ago found women don't want to be very young—our ideal age is closer to forty than to eighteen. And our research finds that women are less likely to think in stereotypes than men are . . . and less likely to think in negative stereotypes when we do. So let me tell you the Truth About Women.

Georgia Hope Witkin, Ph.D.
New York City
May 1995

The
TRUTH
ABOUT
Women

INTRODUCTION

We may think we've moved far beyond the myths of our grandmothers' time, think we've taught our sons and daughters the truth about women, and really believe we've liberated ourselves from preconceived notions, but our Truth About Women research says otherwise. We found:

- Many gender stereotypes still exist.
- The most widely held generalizations are those about women.
- The firmest believers in the stereotypes are men.
- The most frequently endorsed stereotypes about women are mostly negative.

The information came from four sources:

1. Clinical interviews. First, reports by my associates at the Mount Sinai School of Medicine Stress Program in New York City led to the compilation of a list of forty-five gender stereotypes that had been creating personal or interpersonal problems among clients during the past five years. Since a patient population doesn't represent the general population, of course, the list was considered only the starting point.

2. Local surveys. Nonpatient populations were then polled and interviewed through the courtesy of medical centers and universities throughout the country. The almost 4,000 respondents were frequently guests at public seminars and lectures about health and fitness, and were asked to indicate which of the stereotypes they thought were probably true. From these results the fourteen most frequently believed stereotypes discussed in this book were chosen.

Since the local surveys group was self-selected, not random, it's important to understand that the group was fairly representative of the country in terms of age, geographical distribution, occupation, and marital status.

The ages ranged from twenty-one to seventy-two, with 83 percent of the group falling between the ages of twenty-four and sixty-six. The majority of these respondents were female (72 percent).

Geographical distribution ranked according to frequency was:

California	Arizona
New York	Massachusetts
Washington, D.C.	Alabama
Maryland	Mississippi
Illinois	Pennsylvania
Texas	Maine
Connecticut	Colorado
Florida	New Jersey
Ohio	

The occupations most frequently listed were:

teacher	registered nurse
secretary	police officer
counselor	bank teller
office manager	waitress
student	medical
homemaker	technician

education specialist (learning disability, foreign language, attention deficit hyperactivity disorder)

(least frequently mentioned: lobbyist, magician, and cartoonist— one each)

And the marital status closely reflects the national distribution:

55 percent married

23 percent single, never married

16 percent currently divorced

.06 percent widowed

3. *National computer-based survey*. To confirm that the fourteen stereotypes most frequently believed by the local surveys group are also generally believed in other populations, too, PRODIGY computer service offered users a chance to participate in a national poll on gender stereotypes designed for *The Truth About Women*. The PRODIGY Poll appeared on the PRODIGY service between January 13 and February 3, 1995; 14,070 PRODIGY members responded. The fourteen myths about women discussed in this book were listed, and participants were asked to read each and to check "yes" if they believed it, or "no" if they didn't.

The population that responded was 70 percent male and 30 percent female (the reverse of the non-computer-based group in the local polls). The marital status for the 1,439 women looked like this:

37 percent single

52 percent married

9 percent divorced

1.5 percent widowed

The marital status for the men:

29 percent single

63 percent married

7 percent divorced

1 percent widowed

The majority of the group as a whole were in executive/managerial/professional occupations (55 percent). Eleven percent were in sales, support, or clerical jobs, 8 percent worked in service occupations, and 5 percent work with their hands in crafts or mechanical repair or construction. Only 2 percent were laborers or machinists, and 19 percent didn't fit any of these categories.

The age ranges for the group were:

1,987 under twenty-five years old (14 percent).

6,101 twenty-five through forty-four years old (42 percent).

5,986 forty-five years old and older (42 percent).

And their location distribution was rounded off to:

23 percent South

21 percent Midwest

18 percent Pacific

18 percent Northeast

14.5 percent Mid-Atlantic

5 percent Mountain

The results confirmed the non-computer-based local polls and added more detailed information. The details are presented throughout the book, but here are some of the more dramatic summaries:

↠ *Of the fourteen stereotypes about women, the ones* **most commonly believed** *by the group as a whole are:*

Women wish they were young (84 percent).

Women are more romantic than men (73 percent).

Most women want to be married (64 percent).

Most women aren't very mechanical (55 percent).

Women are too emotional (55 percent).

Women have a self-esteem problem (53 percent).

Women have more difficulty than men in midlife (50 percent).

•• *The stereotypes that the* **men and women differed** *most strongly on were:*

Women aren't very mechanical (men are 37 percent more likely than women to agree with this).

Women are the frailer sex (men are 31 percent more likely than women to agree).

Women are too emotional (31 percent more men than women agree, again).

"Vanity, thy name is woman" (26 percent more men than women said yes).

Women make worse bosses (men are 21 percent more likely to agree).

The three items the *men endorsed* most frequently were:

Women wish they were young (87 percent).

Women aren't mechanical (67 percent).

Women are too emotional (65 percent).

(By the way, the majority of the women also thought most women probably want to stay young, but almost 70 percent of women disagree with the idea that women aren't mechanical and 67 percent disagree that women are too emotional.)

•• *The three items about themselves the* **women endorsed** *most frequently were:*

Women wish they were young (78 percent).

Women are more romantic than men (77 percent).

Women have more self-esteem problems (55 percent).

(But women under twenty-five were less likely to think stereotypically than women over twenty-five years old.)

↣ *And the stereotypes* women *most strongly* rejected *were:*

Women aren't interested in sex (87 percent).

Mothers make children neurotic (83 percent).

Women and money are soon parted (82 percent).

Women make worse bosses (80 percent).

4. In-depth interviews. One hundred sixty-six men and women involved with the media (newspapers, radio, television, theater) were asked to go beyond yes and no answers and to elaborate on the stereotypes—to describe each and give examples from our pop culture. Those descriptions are at the beginning of each chapter.

The images they gave of the fourteen myths were vivid, recognizable, and would be believable if I had not spent the past seven years, four days a week, reviewing the latest statistics, surveys, and studies about men and women in order to prepare my television segments for WNBC. Again and again, I was astounded by what I was reading. The truth was often nothing like our assumptions. For example, we talk about holiday depression every year, but national statistics tell us the suicide rate and hospital admissions for depression are somewhat *lower* during the holidays (watch out during February and March, however). Or we talk about only-children having a tough time relating to other children, but the data show they tend to be very popular, class officers, and even more social than children used to fighting for attention with siblings.

Of course, to me, the most astounding of all were the data on women . . . liberating, refreshing, logical data. These findings tell us we are not driven to distraction by our appearance or made emotional cripples by our mothers or society. These findings are compatible with what I see in my office—that women are strong and resilient and motivated not by masochism but by attempts to make their world better. Like men, we wire the lamps and repair the deck. Like men, we worry more about money than vanity and link our self-esteem to our salary if we work.

But my mother, who's a professor of psychiatry and a therapist, as I am, wasn't aware of the information in this book. And my best friend, who's a psychotherapist and hospital administrator, wasn't aware of the information I was finding and gathering. And my daughter, who's a law student with graduate work in sociology, wasn't aware of this information. So my guess is that you may not be aware of much of it, either.

I'm happy to bring you *The Truth About Women*. My family, my friends, my patients, my television viewers, and I myself are now making use of this information . . . and I'll help you make use of it, too!

CHAPTER 1

The Myth:

"Women have a self-esteem problem"

The Myth:

- Women love men who hate them.
- We see only our cellulite when we look in the mirror.
- We shop or eat or both to compensate for feelings of inferiority.
- When we think about careers, our goals are too low because we underrate our intelligence.
- We don't like ourselves, so we don't expect anyone else to like us.
- We don't treat ourselves well because we aren't one of our own loved ones.
- We're threatened by other women, younger women, more beautiful women.

Who Believes It?

Our PRODIGY Poll finds that men and women buy into this myth equally. Exactly 53 percent of men and 53 percent of women say they've heard that women have low self-esteem and believe it's so!

And the *younger* you are, the more *likely* you are to think women have greater self-esteem problems than men. Yet this is the generation raised by more working mothers than any other generation . . . women who, statistics say, are less likely to believe this myth than their own children! The source of influence must be more media than mother. Whereas 57 percent of young men and women under twenty-five years of age agreed with the statement, 53 percent of respondents thirty-five to forty-four years old agreed, and for the over-forty group the rate dropped to a little over 51 percent. Not a great difference, but a clear trend.

Although where we live and what we do for a living seem to make no difference when we look at how men and women together responded to this question (most answered yes, women have a self-esteem problem, regardless of whether they were single, married, divorced, separated, or widowed), when we look at women respondents separately, we find some dramatic differences:

Of the women who work as machinists, laborers, or handlers, *almost all* (91 percent) say they think women have a self-esteem problem, compared to 61 percent of women who work in sales, support, or clerical jobs, 56 percent of women in executive, managerial, or professional occupations, and only 50 percent of women in service, crafts, mechanical repair, or construction areas.

Even more dramatic is the finding that only 62 percent of the men who work in the same occupations (as machinists, laborers, or handlers) said yes, they think women have a self-esteem problem. We can't be sure if the high percentage of those who subscribe to the myth among women machinists, laborers, and handlers reflects actual lower self-esteem among women in more routinized jobs than in the other occupations or just more of a tendency to use this explanation for negative feelings. Either way, this chapter can help!

Who said no to this myth most frequently? Among women, wise

widows (43 percent)! Among men, it was the divorced and separated (43 percent).

Now let's see if the non-computer-based local surveys group agrees with the PRODIGY Poll. Not surprisingly, this group gave responses that basically followed the same pattern. Twenty-seven percent more men than women said that they have heard, and believe, that men have better self-esteem. The quotes went like this:

Female, thirty-seven years old: "Isn't low self-esteem the reason I blame myself for everything?"

Male, forty-two years old: "Every magazine cover I see at the supermarket is telling women how to improve their self-esteem, so they must have a problem with it. I never hear guys talking about self-esteem." (I asked him if this means men don't have a self-esteem problem. He said, "It means we never think about it one way or the other.")

Female, forty-eight years old: "I think African-Americans like myself hear white people talking about low self-esteem among blacks, and so now I worry about it, too."

Female, sixty-two years old: "My mother never spoke to me about low self-esteem. My forty-year-old daughter sure does."

The Truth

It may be *popular* to say that we have low self-esteem and therefore we have low career expectations, high stress levels, and depression, but it's *not true* generally. Self-esteem is usually defined as a favorable impression of oneself, a feeling of worth . . . and more than ever, women seem to like themselves and how they look and feel.

➻ *Most women are satisfied with their level of self-esteem.* According to the Replens Report, a 1993 nationwide survey of 1,014 adult women commissioned by the Parke-Davis Pharmaceutical Company, 91 percent of women are *not* dissatisfied with their level of self-esteem. In fact, satisfaction among women is nearly equal to that of men (95 percent). More than half the women in the survey (52 percent) are "very satisfied" with their level of self-esteem.

↳ ***Most women (89 percent) aren't dissatisfied with their attractiveness,*** according to the same report. That's just four percentage points below men in the same sample. The difference used to be greater—we typically rated our looks below average and men rated theirs above. But no longer. We may read about diets, sign up for exercise classes, want to improve, buy control-top stockings, and complain a lot, but nearly nine women in ten are happy enough with their appearance.

This study showed we now parallel men in one other way, too: Our self-esteem is linked more to salary than to appearance. Unfortunately, the glass ceiling, above which are the rarefied salaries, has very few cracks: Only 6 percent of Fortune 1,000 directorships, for example, are held by women. Pay is better but still not equal, with female salaries now averaging 70 percent of those of men. So when it comes to how we feel about ourselves, statistics seem to say that it's not our looks, our appearance, our men, or how well we're liked that strains our self-esteem. It's our financial concern. It's as if we're saying, "Give me the money my work is worth, in and out of the home, and I'll handle the rest!"

↳ ***Women's and men's self-esteem is equally vulnerable.*** Fifty-three percent of women and 50 percent of men report that life events such as divorce, illness, financial loss, or failure at work weakened their self-confidence, according to the Keri Report, a study of 1,002 women and 251 men, sponsored by Westwood Pharmaceuticals in 1988.

↳ ***American women describe themselves as self-assured.*** A new "Secret" survey of 500 women commissioned by Procter & Gamble found that more than 85 percent of women respondents say they're self-assured. The study also found that 95 percent of women credit their family with building up their inner strength.

↳ ***The majority of women say they like themselves,*** and . . .

↳ ***say they are intelligent.*** According to the Keri Report, 61 percent of women said they like themselves, and 55 percent said they think they are intelligent.

↝ *Women earn more than half of all associate, bachelor's, and master's degrees,* and . . .

↝ *Women receive almost half of all doctorates and medical and law degrees,* according to Clifford Adelman, senior research analyst for the U.S. Department of Education. He calls women "the greatest success story in higher education of the past twenty-five years."

But what about teenage girls? Do they have a self-esteem problem? Reports by the American Association of University Women (AAUW) in 1991 and 1992 discovered that classroom teachers are more likely to ignore girls than boys, and that many textbooks are biased against females. Could these factors contribute to a dramatic drop in the self-esteem of schoolgirls?

Many experts in adolescent development don't believe so. Diane Ravitch, Ph.D., former assistant secretary of education and now senior research scholar at New York University, points out in *Working Mother* magazine that even if teachers call on boys more, it's not clear that this helps the boys:

↝ *More adult men than women lack a high school diploma.*

↝ *Fewer young men go for the degree.* Young men have lower educational aspirations.

↝ *Boys usually earn lower report-card grades.*

↝ *Teenage girls generally have a higher opinion of themselves as learners than boys,* according to a 1993 study of 400 sixth- through eighth-graders by the University of North Carolina at Greensboro.

↝ *More girls than boys feel the teacher is interested in them,* according to a U.S. Department of Education study of 25,000 eighth-through tenth-graders.

↝ *Seventy-two percent of girls (but only 68 percent of boys) said teachers listened to what they had to say,* according to the same study. In fact, critics of the AAUW study pointed out that the differences in the way boys and girls were treated added up to a lag, not a deficit; and boys may get more attention from teachers only because they're more unruly. But the study *has* had some positive effects. Tests and texts have been revised, and more teachers have sensitized themselves to the issues and have begun to share their attention equally with girls and boys.

↦ ***Girls' aspirations are more realistic than those of boys.*** It seems the often cited conclusion of many researchers that boys have higher career aspirations than girls may have more to do with unrealistic expectations than with self-esteem. According to the AAUW data, girls' number-one aspiration is to become a lawyer—a dream less glamorous and more realistic than boys' dreams of being a rock star or sports star, and more likely a measure of earlier maturity than lower self-regard. So why do many observers say teenage girls often act as if they're more insecure than boys? Some researchers suggest that boys *seem* to have higher self-esteem because they hide their insecurities behind bragging. Many others suggest that teen boys and girls have equal doubt and self-consciousness, but girls are better at expressing these feelings.

How to Use the Truth

The myth of low self-esteem implies that many of the difficulties of life in the nineties for women are our own doing. But this conclusion blames the victim. The high divorce rate, crime level, drug presence, economic depression, and glass ceiling are not functions of our self-esteem, they batter our self-esteem. In the seventies, trend watchers reported that we lost our extended families as neighborhoods changed, mobility increased, and parents, in-laws, and even grandparents divorced. In the late eighties, financial experts said we lost our hopes of upward mobility, savings, and security as a recession and inflation hit at the same time. In the nineties, sociologists say, we fill more roles, as more than 90 percent of women will have to work at some point in their lives, and more than 50 percent will have to be single parents as well. We haven't run out of self-esteem, we've run out of family, money, and time.

We are feeling tired, worried, and alone, and then blaming ourselves for feeling that way.

We are feeling out of control, and then saying the cause is low self-esteem.

We're told that we must first have self-esteem to treat ourselves with esteem. But that's one more myth. *The truth about self-esteem is that self-esteem can be the* result *of how we treat ourselves, not just the cause.* That means if you didn't receive esteem as a gift from your parents when you were young, you can give it to yourself now. That means if your self-esteem gets lowered or drops, you can get it back. And that means if your self-esteem is fine but you want more of a good thing, you can boost it even more. Here's how to do all three.

↤ *Parent yourself.* If your parents didn't teach you how to treat yourself with esteem, it's time to parent yourself. I first discussed the concept of self-parenting in *The Female Stress Syndrome.* I suggested that we parent ourselves as we parent others. That means watching our sleep, exercise, and nutrition with the same concern and attention we show toward our children, mates, parents, friends, and pets . . . not necessarily more, but certainly not less. It means declaring a mental health day and not contaminating it with chores; sending the children out to play and joining them; getting educational degrees; taking time to practice religion, if we choose; or taking charge of our appearance. That's how parents give their children esteem. That's how you can start to give it to yourself.

↤ *Know yourself.* If your parents didn't really get to know you, if they were more focused on who they wanted you to be than who you are, it's time to know yourself.

At the top of a sheet of paper, write the following incomplete sentence: "I am someone who _____." Complete the sentence in a new and different way each day. It will force you to collect information on yourself. If you write in "too tidy" or "overly sensitive," cross out "too" and "overly." This is a nonjudgmental exercise in self-knowledge, not self-improvement. List all traits, not just the "good" ones: "I am someone who gets sleepy when I am anxious," or, "I am someone who loves a competitive game," or, "I am someone who would rather exercise than diet," etc. You will soon know who you are, not who others say you are or who they think you should be. My patients have done this exercise for years and have come to accept themselves as a mixed bag . . . as we all are.

↤ *Anticipate drops.* Next, although most women don't have the kind of self-esteem problem people think we do, our self-esteem *can* drop.

—Self-esteem usually drops when our self-expectations are unrealistically high, because we become self-critical.

—Self-esteem can drop during periods of change like divorce or a move (or even a good change like marriage or promotion), because our sense of control erodes and we aren't sure we can deal with the unexpected.

—Self-esteem may drop when we fail to excel at work or are victims of sexual harassment, because we first review all our own behavior to see if we could have prevented the outcome before we accept the facts as they are and move on.

—Self-esteem frequently drops when a woman is abused by her spouse or partner. But it's usually not low self-esteem that keeps her in an abusive situation. And it's usually not because she believes she deserves the abuse. Most often it's because women feel they have no other options—no money, no job, no place to go with the children—or are afraid the abuser will find them and punish them for leaving.

—Self-esteem always drops if we overschedule ourselves to the point that we ruin our sleep, neglect our body, eat poorly, and postpone our talents because we're waiting for the day when we're all caught up. If we neglect ourselves, we'll feel neglected. If we put ourselves last, we'll begin to feel that we come last.

But the good news is that we can get self-esteem back as often as it's lowered or lost. The key, once again, is that when we choose to act with self-esteem, we begin to *feel* self-esteem.

↔ *Choose your thoughts and behavior.* Perhaps the most useful finding within the world of psychotherapy in the past two decades is that our feelings can follow from our behavior as well as the other way around. So if you're feeling low on self-esteem, don't go with the flow. Don't withdraw from your friends or you'll have no reminders that you are valued by others. Don't stop exercising, doing chores, and working or you'll be telling your body its strength isn't needed. Don't change your schedule, or your biological clock will run down and sleeping and eating habits will change.

Instead, *do* talk to yourself as if your self-esteem is still high. If someone has treated you badly, ask yourself what that tells you about *them,* not you. If you've brought your own self-esteem down by not excelling as much as you wanted to, either readjust your expectations or keep trying if it's realistic.

When others try to choose our thoughts for us by reminding us how much worse things could be, or telling us how lucky we are, it's rarely very effective. But research is clear that telling ourselves the very same things is effective.

↦ *Pause and pace yourself.* Most of us leave no time in our day for ourselves. This isn't masochism. This is a misguided notion that we can catch up with the demands of all our roles if we do more and more. Women tell me they learned from their mothers that they should take care of everyone and everything else first, and use the leftover time to recharge their own self-esteem. But there is *no more leftover time!* In fact, a survey I helped to design for the 1991 Bristol-Myers Keri Report found we're all running on a time deficit. We asked women to add up the time they needed to take care of their job, family, finances, and chores, and subtract the time they were awake each day. Most women found they were running an average of *twenty-one minutes short a day!*

So don't wait for leftover time. And try to be realistic, because when we take care of everyone and everything else before we get to our own needs, we fail doubly. We won't always please everyone else and we won't take care of ourselves either. Set some priorities and schedule some rest pauses into the day. (See Chapter 3 for some ways that a chronically busy woman can take breaks.) And don't tell yourself you can't make time for yourself. Research by Herbert Benson, M.D., of Harvard University, concludes that we need at least twenty minutes a day of relaxation to help prevent stress symptoms and stress-related illness. So if you don't take at least a total of twenty minutes a day for personal downtime, you'll probably be stuck with downtime anyway, but it won't be the kind you can use to confirm your self-esteem. It will be downtime to treat a migraine, flu, or a strained back. The moral? I'm not saying self-esteem requires us to put ourselves above our loved ones. But I am saying self-esteem means including ourselves on our list of loved ones.

↦ *Accept yourself.* No one is perfect. We aren't supposed to be perfect, and I frequently tell my patients that it's mental cruelty to expect ourselves or anyone else to be perfect.

↦ *Credit yourself.* Research indicates that some women tend to blame themselves when something goes wrong and thank their lucky stars when it goes right, whereas most men credit themselves when something goes right and blame bad luck when it doesn't. Let's take a lesson from men! Next time you're faced with success, *take credit.* Then give yourself a pat on the back and tell at least one other person.

When something is wrong, see it as an "inconvenience"—as a fact, not a fault. For example, a committee or board you head is making no progress because members are feuding. See it as a problem to be corrected, an inconvenience, a fact, not a reason to torture yourself with blame or feel insecure. A restaurant or movie you chose was awful? "Inconvenient," not a tragedy.

↦ *Manage shyness.* Many women confuse shyness with lack of self-esteem, but low self-esteem is more often the result rather than the cause of shyness. Most shy people didn't start out with a self-esteem problem; it came after shyness interfered with risk-taking, exploration, and interaction with people who might have built self-esteem. In fact, some experts believe shyness is a genetic inclination (see Chapter 8, page 102). But that doesn't mean it can't be recognized and overcome! There are many ways to fight "party panic," "speaker's shakes," and other forms of shyness:

—First, go out when it would feel better to stay in. Make it a goal to speak with just one person; at the next gathering, speak with two people, and so on. This change in behavior tells your nervous system that anxiety and other warning signals are going to be ignored—soon they are no longer produced.

—Then, when you come face-to-face with someone new in a social setting and feel at a loss, extend your hand and introduce yourself. Odds are that the other person will return the courtesy of an introduction. What next? Ask a question, especially if an awkward moment is coming on. At an office party you can ask, "Where did you work before?" At a dinner party try, "How do you know our host?" Keep the other person talking until you begin to relax.

—To keep others in conversation, lean forward to close out other conversations going on around you. Nod to show sympathy. Mirror the frowns and smiles of the other person to show empathy.

—When it is time to talk, trade basic information that matches information received—for example, where you live, what you do.

—If you haven't given a speech or stood up for your rights yet, practice on friends or family, where you know you'll find compassion and tolerance. Your feelings of shyness may never fade entirely, but your shy behavior will. And practice in acting un-shy can help.

—And, most important of all, wait for a comfortable feeling *before* leaving a gathering. If you leave in the midst of anxiety symptoms and then your anxiety goes down, you've just rewarded yourself for escaping. You'll be more likely to run away again in the future!

↔ ***Don't be bullied.*** If others—boss, spouse, children—try to bully you into believing you should be perfect, don't take it. Bullies are always looking for psychological games they can win. We have to let them know we aren't playing.

Next time a parent criticizes you in front of your children, or a spouse or a supervisor shouts at you in public, give a firm answer, eye-to-eye, to show that you are not intimidated.

If the explosion is part of a conversation, go back to that exact flash point in the discussion where the tantrum started, to show that the tantrum won't work as an evasion tactic.

For example, you are talking with a colleague about a personnel decision. The colleague then takes a call, becomes agitated, slams down the phone, walks back to your desk, and snarls, "Women like you are too soft-hearted when it comes to personnel decisions."

What should you do? Don't be defensive; this only gives the bully an excuse to keep arguing. And if you're emotional, this will only make the bully feel more powerful. Instead, the rule is, "No reaction, no satisfaction." Return to the flash point where he or she blew up, and calmly and evenly say, "In this case what we're talking about is . . ." then reiterate.

If none of these tactics works and you're still being bullied, excuse yourself and leave the room. Forget about winning and losing. Forget about appearances, and walk away. You can't be a victim if you aren't there!

↔ *Assert yourself.* When it comes to signing up for assertiveness-training courses, women still outnumber men about four to one. That's probably because many women get so much "non-assertiveness training" when they're young and praised for being sweet, pretty, nurturing, and cooperative. These are all good traits, but being able to express opinions and set limits are important skills, too. So here are some practice assignments to help increase your assertiveness.

—Make eye contact and keep it. When we don't focus on the person we're talking to, we're more likely to start focusing on ourselves and how we sound, and that can cause self-consciousness. If long periods of eye contact are too uncomfortable, you can just focus on the bridge of the nose—it's usually read as eye contact.

—Use statements that begin with "I" instead of "you" (such as, "I get upset when I have to wait a long time," rather than, "You don't care if you keep me waiting"). This type of statement asserts our feelings but falls short of an attack. (See Chapter 6 for more about emotions.)

—In the event that an assertive approach brings on an argument or resistance, try the "instant replay" technique. Decide on a single sentence that expresses the original request or feeling and then keep repeating it firmly . . . again and again.

↔ *Be a model.* Research says self-esteem can increase a young girl's school performance, improve her relationships, ensure her moral growth, encourage her self-confidence, and even help her enjoy play. So give her a head start. Parents, teachers, aunts, friends, and sisters can encourage young women in the following ways:

—Encourage them to join athletics by being athletic yourself and by attending their events and workouts. Competition, winning, and losing are all skills that build self-esteem. And the muscle tone that exercise gives can make a young woman feel stronger and more fit.

—Teach girls to use computers and encourage them to take science courses. Although girls are now doing both, girls and women have traditionally not been encouraged in these areas. Technology is a key to future employment and also enjoyment.

—Take a young woman to work. Several years ago, the *Ms.* Foundation for Women initiated a "Take Your Daughter to Work" day to give girls a chance to see women functioning successfully in the working world and to raise awareness in the workplace of a girl's need for models. Remember, the "Secret" survey found that 95 percent of working women surveyed said family encouragement was the most important ingredient in building their inner strength. So take the girls in your life to work so they can see confidence in action, networking, women who take chances, take charge, take pride in their career and pride in their appearance. Pick a day to bring a son to work, too. Let him see myths being broken.

—At home, encourage responsibility and independence. Research says that boys are usually encouraged to do more exploring and sent on more errands at earlier ages, punished less for expressing aggression, and encouraged to do more physical activities, while girls are talked to, cuddled more often as infants, and given more compliments on appearance than any other trait as young girls. This isn't new: A classic study from the 1950s found that 82 percent of parents in 110 cultures expected females to be less achieving and less self-reliant than male children. And a reassessment of sex roles and attitudes by social psychologists M. Lewin and L. M. Tragos in 1987 found that adolescent stereotypes of male and female sex roles have not changed substantially in the past twenty-five years! Time for a change.

—Help girls take risks. Encourage them to try things: music, dance, drama, athletics, a new summer camp, a new academic or non-academic study (such as auto mechanics), a different summer job, setting up a lemonade stand, or manning a booth at the school fair. If a girl is fearful, ask her what's the worst that can happen if she fails. The answer is usually "Nothing that can't be handled." Show her by example how to take credit every time her efforts go right, and help her see her failures as life lessons, not embarrassments. Adults need to make sure girls don't feel they must be perfect. Point out the difference between perfect (unreal) and very good or good enough (real). And point out that less than a 25 percent failure rate probably means she's just not taking on enough new challenges.

↔ **Get help for problems.** If self-esteem problems overwhelm you or have led you to drinking, drugs, or depression—three ways some people try to numb emotional pain—please get professional help as fast as possible. Ask your physician for a referral.

COUNTERING THE MYTH OF LOW SELF-ESTEEM

If self-esteem could be higher, here's a boost:

Know yourself. Know who you are, not just who you think you should be.

Accept yourself. You aren't perfect; you aren't supposed to be. To expect to be is mental cruelty!

Credit yourself. When things go well, pat yourself on the back and tell at least one other person.

Parent yourself. If your parents didn't give you the gift of self-esteem, give it to yourself! When we treat ourselves with respect, we feel respected. When we treat ourselves with love, we feel loved. That's how parents give children self-esteem. That's how we can give it to ourselves.

CHAPTER 2

The Myth:

"Midlife is difficult for women"

The Myth:

- The midlife woman's children are grown and she's broken-hearted.
- Her vision and teeth are going, and so is her memory.
- In the morning, sudden wrinkles.
- In the afternoon, fatigue.
- In the evening, irritability.
- In bed, night sweats.
- No sex drive, no sex appeal, no sex partner.
- It's too late to start a new career and too early to retire.
- She thinks her mate really wants to trade her in.

Who Believes It?

This stereotype separates the "boomers" from the "older" generation and the women from the men. Let's look at the generations first.

The majority of the PRODIGY Poll respondents who say no, they don't think midlife is more difficult for women, are people approaching midlife now (under forty-four years old). They're the youngest of the baby boomers, and they seem to be optimistic or confident or both. The majority of the group that agreed with the statement are forty-five and older. Either the stereotype was more widely held by that group, or midlife really was more difficult for women then compared to now, or both.

Now let's look at gender differences. Although, as a group, half of the respondents agree with the statement (50 percent say yes, 36 percent say no, and 14 percent say not sure), those percentages were heavily influenced by the large number of male responses (they outnumber women more than two to one on this poll). The majority of men certainly think midlife is more difficult for women! Single men, married men, divorced men, and widowers agreed; only 30 percent of male respondents said no to this question.

Most women, on the other hand, seem to know better. The pattern of their response was the reverse of the men's. Only 38 percent said yes, they think midlife is more difficult for women; 52 percent said no, and 10 percent said not sure. This pattern is true for all occupations in all areas of the country. In fact, the only exception to the pattern was among widows. The majority of that group (52 percent) said they agreed with the statement, but single, married, and divorced or separated women did not!

The non-computer-based local surveys parallel the PRODIGY Poll.

More than 81 percent of respondents in the local surveys have heard of the female midlife crisis, but many question it:

Female, age thirty-one: "I think women are less afraid of midlife because they definitely survive loneliness better. My aunt is doing great since my uncle died, but my father's like a little old man."

Female, age fifty-two: "My friends and I were talking . . . [we] think women don't mind reaching the halfway mark because we're less afraid of death than men . . . and less afraid of getting sick . . . maybe less afraid of everything."

Male, age forty-eight: "Men are definitely more scared when it comes to illness. . . ."

Female, age forty-seven: "I'm finally getting respect!"

Female, age forty-two: "The police are all starting to look young. . . . I don't like that!"

Male, age thirty-seven: "Every year, my wife speaks up more, and she's less shy. What's she going to be like when she's in midlife?"

Female, age forty-eight: "I'm not depressed, but I don't like the sagging. I can control everything else but not the sagging."

Female, age twenty-eight: "My boyfriend is beginning to get a little bit bald, and he's already freaking. . . ."

Female, age seventy-four: "Midlife never took me by surprise. I didn't suddenly say, 'Where did the time go?' I always knew where it went. I knew what was happening. It was okay."

Male, age fifty: "We can gain ten pounds or ten years without it making much difference. Women can't."

The Truth

In Grandmother's day, midlife began as soon as the children were out of the house—say, sometime in her thirties! Women married younger, had children more quickly, and usually aged faster. Today, midlife (also known as middle age) is generally defined chronologically by researchers as spanning ages forty-six to sixty-six. A 1994 Clinique-sponsored poll of 1,001 women sixteen years old and over identified the point when a person "stops being young" at age fifty-four. According to a national survey by the American Board of Family Practice, which certifies family physicians, middle age is also a state of mind. We:

—no longer recognize the music groups

—think more about the past than the future

—need a day or two to recover from strenuous exercise

—see our last child move out (now it happens much later)

—worry about having enough money to cover health costs

—become a grandparent, or

—get respect!

Although many of us associate the words "midlife" and "crisis," the truth is that midlife isn't very difficult for most women and can even be the best time of our lives.

↔ *Some things get better.* Just in time for the baby boomers' fiftieth-birthday parties, science says midlife has advantages. In fact, a *Longevity* magazine survey finds some things actually get better with age. Here are a few of their findings:

Migraines become less frequent as hormone levels drop, and some of us outgrow them completely.

Allergies become milder.

Our complexion clears up as skin becomes drier.

The risk of developing manic-depression drops.

Teeth usually become less sensitive as their nerve and blood supply decreases.

Other studies also have some good news about midlife.

↔ *Women often feel more interested in sex.* Some physicians believe that desire may increase because as a woman's estrogen level decreases, she can feel more of the effect of her androgens (testosterone and other male hormones that women have in lower levels than men). Androgens regulate the male sex drive and contribute to libido in women too. As a bonus, we're no longer worried about pregnancy and usually less exhausted from small children. And although a survey called "Is There Sex After 40?" published in *Psychology Today* in the late seventies found 50 percent of all college students think their parents don't make love more than once a month, and 25 percent guess once a year, current surveys say it's more like once or twice a week!

↔ *Married couples get happier.* In general, surveys find that if a woman marries young and stays married, marital happiness improves with every year after the first twenty-five . . . and so does sexual satisfaction! Couples say it's because most women find they have more time, most children are out of the house, and most men focus more on leisurely lovemaking.

↔ *Sex remains frequent.* The 1994 *Parade* magazine "Sex in America" survey found that men and women fifty-five to sixty-five make love an average of five times a month (as often as single people). *The Janus Report*, by Samuel S. Janus, Ph.D., and Cynthia L. Janus, M.D., says that 69 percent of men and 74 percent of women over sixty-five report sexual activity at least weekly. And half of women sixty-five and over, and 93 percent of men the same age, say they have frequent orgasms during lovemaking. We never grow too old for love.

↔ *Extramarital affairs are less common.* The 1993 General Social Survey, an annual study of about 1,400 people by the University of Chicago's National Opinion Research Center, found that extramarital affairs are less common among people born before 1940. Is it the fear of AIDS that keeps potential wanderers closer to home? Experts say, probably not as much *as it should*. It's more likely the values that generation holds. And people who live in the country, attend church, and have never been divorced have the fewest extramarital affairs of all. By the way, income levels seem to make no difference, although we used to think that the more money you earned, the higher risk you were for an affair.

↔ *The risk of depression may drop in midlife.* Midlife isn't linked with depression, according to two Columbia University studies. In the first, a ten-year study of 511 women in Connecticut, depression was most likely around age thirty-five and *dropped as the women got older*, according to Myrna Weissman, M.D., and her team. The surprised researchers thought a larger follow-up study was in order; a poll of 18,000 women in five urban areas confirmed their first findings.

What about the midlife crisis? Surely that plunges both men and women into a well of dark despair? Not so, say psychologists and my own patients. The so-called midlife crisis can occur at any age, whenever we search for meaning, intimacy, and purpose. The data show that middle age is the very best time in life, says Ronald Kessler, Ph.D., a sociologist at the University of Michigan's Institute for Social Research, and our interviewees agree. They say they don't have the physical problems of old age yet and they've left many anxieties of youth behind. They know who loves them, and their career is in full swing. Rates of depression and anxiety fall at about thirty-five and don't climb again until the late sixties. You usually have enough money to do some of the things you'd like to do. You've usually worked out relationships with family members, and the chance of divorce, as we've said, is very low. You are officially a "grown-up" but may still feel like a kid. It's a time to enjoy.

↔ *Many women enjoy an empty nest.* Of course, a woman whose family has been everything to her may become depressed when the children grow up and away. It's the end of life as she knows it. However, it's also the beginning of a new life, so not every mother is devastated by the departure of her grown children—some mothers even smile as they wave good-bye!

In fact, a study from one of my alma maters, Wellesley, researched more than 200 women aged thirty-five to fifty-five and showed that 74 percent of women whose children had left were *relieved, happy, even delighted!* Their feelings of self-worth were higher than they had been during the child-rearing period. It's potentially a time of opportunity, time to resume a career, rekindle romance, recapture enthusiasm for hobbies and activities that have been sidelined for years. A researcher who looked at the working lives of 150 people found that the years from age sixty-five to 102 were just as active as the years before. The best thing about midlife is "being settled," said 39 percent of women and 50 percent of men in a study by the American Board of Family Practice. We usually know who we are, what we like, and where we want to live.

↔ *Few women are drastically sandwiched.* One main challenge during the midlife years may be taking care of elderly parents. In the American Board of Family Practice study, four out of five people forty-six and younger agreed that children have an obligation to care for their parents until the parents die. This can be a stress, especially a financial one if the "sandwich generation" is paying for college *and* a nursing home.

But the truth about the sandwich generation is that very few people are caught caring for two generations—the younger and the older—at the same time. Research from the State University of New York at Albany finds that middle-aged people don't usually become involved in taking care of an elderly parent (usually a mother who is now a widow) until after the children are much older and need less time and attention.

When the time does come to care for an elderly parent, these suggestions from lawyers, physicians, and social workers can make life easier. If you are parenting a parent:

—Set up files listing important phone numbers and the location of important papers: medical records, wills, bank books. The files shouldn't contain the actual documents, just their locations.

—Do a safety check of your parents' residence. Make sure there are night-lights in the hallways, no-slip treads and grab bars in the shower, and smoke alarms and fire extinguishers that work. Clear paths so walking areas are free of cords, shoes, and anything else that could cause a fall. Put slippery throw rugs into storage.

—Visit or call your parents' physician to find out about medications, dosages, side effects.

—Offer choices whenever possible. *Science* offers a review of more than sixty studies showing an increase in optimism and health and a decrease in complaints of pain in elderly people given a *choice* about daily life such as movies, menus, and the type of plant in their room.

—Remember that he or she will probably want some privacy and independence.

And most of all, older parents say they need dignity and respect. Ask for their opinion or help with decisions, and then remember to thank them for it.

Finally, the "children" must remember to look after their own needs, too. Caring for elderly people is a gift of love, but be loving with yourself, too, or you'll burn out. When the work becomes tiresome or "too much," ask for help or take a break. You're entitled to laugh and have some fun even if your parent can't.

↬ *Menopause isn't a universal agony.* The research is clear: Most women deal well with menopause. A survey for *Working Woman* magazine found that although 55 percent of women expected to be depressed during their menopause, only 10 percent actually were. The Massachusetts Women's Health Study found the majority of women report relief or feeling neutral about losing their menstruation . . . and the feelings become more positive as they actually experience menopause. And a study of 15,000 women, directed by researchers at the Center for Women's Health at Columbia-Presbyterian Medical Center in New York, turned up these numbers:

—58 percent called menopause "somewhat bothersome."

—More than half of respondents say symptoms are mild.

—For every woman who finds menopause truly traumatic, another woman sails through it with no physical or emotional storms *at all.*

Menopause can, however, be an inconvenience! We tend to gain weight, for example: A 1994 study of 15,000 readers of *Prevention* magazine found that more than half of women gained at least ten pounds during menopause. Some menopause symptoms—vaginal dryness, skin changes, unpredictable moods—can be *major* inconveniences. In the same study, 40 percent of women reported hot flashes, and 62 percent of those women said the hot flashes came at night, interrupting sleep.

The women who have the least trouble with menopause are the ones who counter it with action, according to a survey of 500 women by Karen Matthews, M.D., a professor of psychiatry, epidemiology, and psychology at the University of Pittsburgh School of Medicine. These women tend to exercise more or try hormones or both. They get double benefits: the benefit of the exercise and hormones *and* the benefit of an increased sense of control just when their body is changing.

If you're worried that menopause will make you less sexy and sexual, you're not alone: A Gallup Poll found that 45 percent of men and 23 percent of women were worried that menopause would ruin their sex lives. But *after* the women reached menopause, 61 percent of the men and 70 percent of the women said there was *no change at all.*

↔ *Aging can improve intimacy.* In medical fact, sex may improve as the partners age. The reasons sex improves are several:

As men age, they need more manual stimulation to get an erection, so women feel more needed, and ejaculatory urgency diminishes, so premature ejaculation is less likely and foreplay can be extended.

And as women age, many shed lingering hangups and guilt about sex. In fact, a woman in her sixties who has not been orgasmic before may experience her first orgasm now. And as couples age together, the affection and intimacy they enjoy may even grow stronger, according to a Boston study of people aged eighteen to eighty-five. (For a closer look at the midlife woman's sexuality, see Chapter 4.)

↔ *Divorce isn't always a disaster.* Though some women who divorce in midlife may be desperately searching for another man, a Long Island University study of 352 midlife women found that three divorced women in four have no wish to remarry—they value their independence and privacy too much to cede it to a man again! Four women in five feel they have a more positive self-image and higher self-esteem, too. Two women out of three say the divorce helped them get control over their lives for the first time. One in four divorced women says sex is better after the split!

In truth, divorce is less common during this time anyway. Most couples break up in the first six or eight years of the marriage; if they've made it past ten or fifteen years, chances are they'll make it through the next ten or fifteen. And the middle-aged philanderer, it turns out, is as mythical as the sexless middle-aged woman. A study by John McKinlay found that only 2 percent of the 1,700 middle-aged men he studied reported having more than one current sexual partner.

How to Use the Truth

Midlife is filled with changes. Don't confuse them with losses. Most of us adjust quickly to the changes that midlife brings. The vehicle is action:

↠ *Take your life back.* If you've been a full-time parent or full-time worker for the last twenty years or so, the midlife years are a chance to shift the focus more to yourself. Make them a time for growth, a time to think thoughts that are new. Take another look at your love partner—who may seem like a stranger—and renew your friendship again. It may also be time to return to the "working world" if you left it, if you're bored, if you're broke.

↠ *Eliminate barriers to good sex.* Our sexual life is part desire, part opportunity, part arousal, part orgasm, and part satisfaction. A problem in any one of these stages can keep us from moving on to the next. The most common reasons for sexual dysfunction in women are hormonal changes, depression or past depression, medication side effects, vaginal infections or surgery that makes intercourse painful, drug abuse, and illness. All of these can be eliminated or dealt with (see Chapter 4).

↠ *Get more exercise.* Exercise is the original fountain of youth if ever there was one. Moderate exercise can:

—help keep your heart and lungs strong by increasing their efficiency

—keep joints flexible by using them

—maintain bone strength through stimulation

—improve alertness by encouraging blood circulation to the brain

—stimulate the immune system

—help stave off or control some of the diseases of aging: diabetes, hypertension, dangerous blood fat levels

—relieve some menopause symptoms

In the *Prevention* magazine study, women who said menopause was "not bothersome" exercised three times a week or more, but only 39 percent of women who exercised two or fewer times a week could say the same. And a Swedish study of 634 women found that 25 percent of sedentary women had "severe" hot flashes; only 6 percent of exercisers did. As a bonus, we can count on the slimmer, trimmer body and healthy glow that come from regular workouts. Exercise can not only give us a more fit body but the energy to enjoy it, too.

↠ *Consider the hormone option.* A Gallup poll indicates that about 30 percent of menopausal women use hormone replacement therapy (HRT). Although it's usually prescribed to prevent some form of heart disease and/or osteoporosis, maintaining your estrogen levels as your ovaries begin to produce less and less has other benefits, too. For as long as it's taken, HRT can control hot flashes, cold sweats, vaginal dryness, mood swings, and perhaps, say new studies, even some short-term memory loss. Add some replacement testosterone and research finds a low-level libido may become more active again. Check with your physician, however, because HRT is by prescription and certainly not for everyone. For example, it's not usually recommended for women with high risk of breast cancer. For these women there are over-the-counter vaginal lubricants for vaginal dryness, a low-salt diet for water retention, drinking less alcohol for hot flashes, meditation for anxiety, and more. Again, check with your physician for options.

↠ *Make your dreams come true.* Until midlife, we may have postponed our dreams: no money for the boat we wanted, no time to learn a musical instrument, no support for going back to school. With luck, fewer barriers may stand in the way. Now our job may be less demanding, or we may need less money and cut back to part-time work.

Now our spouse may more comfortable with, or at least less threatened by, our outside interests and the absences they require. Our children may be grown and no longer take so much of our time and resources, so we may actually feel more energetic and more interested in pursuing new studies or travel. It's time, finally, for some fun.

It's also time to know which dreams will probably not come true, to go around barriers instead of hitting your head against them or tripping over them! If the money for the boat still isn't there, rent one for the season. If you've wanted to be a concert pianist but don't have the talent, teach or perform for charity. Now's the time to see who you really are, enjoy who you are.

•• *Choose whom you compare yourself to.* Make it fair, realistic, and complimentary. Or don't compare yourself to others at all.

COUNTERING THE MYTH OF MIDLIFE MISERY

Contrary to what we hear, midlife generally isn't a time of crisis for women. Some do have life crises during midlife, but *no more than have crises at other times.* Here's what to remember about midlife:

Midlife is a time of psychological reorganization, as are other times of life. But this reorganization is one you can shape.

Midlife is a time of physical change, as are other times of life. *Don't confuse change with loss!* Exercise and preventive medical care can keep you in shape.

Midlife is a time of maturity and self-knowledge. Enjoy it.

CHAPTER 3

The Myth:

"Women are not achievement-oriented"

The Myth:

- Women don't have the competitiveness men do.
- Women don't mind waiting as much as men do.
- Women are less critical and perfectionist.
- Women collapse under pressure.
- Women are uncomfortable asking for a raise.
- Women work for self-fulfillment, not success.
- We'd rather avoid confrontation . . .
- We'd rather be liked.

Who Believes It?

For the past twenty years, achievement-driven and success-oriented people have been referred to as "Type A personalities," and that's the label we used in our survey. One out of three men (35 percent) agrees that women are less likely to be Type A personalities. Fewer women believe this one. Just 17 percent of women in our computer sample gave a yes answer to this question.

Age influences responses here. The older you are, the more you seem to agree with the myth. One out of three men and women over the age of forty-five (37 percent) say women *are* less likely to be Type A. The number drops to about 27 percent for those between twenty-five and forty-four, and to just 16 percent for those under twenty-five.

Regarding marital status, divorced and separated women believe it the most among females (26 percent). This compares to 21 percent among married women and 14 percent among singles. Divorced and separated men answer yes 41 percent of the time, compared to 39 percent for married and 27 percent for single men.

The non-computer-based local surveys found that men and women both say that men feel anger more intensely and that makes men more Type A.

And from the interviews, here are representative quotes:

Male, age fifty-five: "Women are less likely to be Type A's because men are more aggressive by nature."

Female, age forty-eight: "I'm as aggravated by incompetence as any guy. I end up by doing everything myself—that's Type A!"

Female, age twenty-four: "I think my mother's a Type A . . . more than my father. But she's a housewife, so it's not so obvious."

Female, age seventy-two: "I'm a perfectionist, I make lists, I can't stand not being busy . . . if that's a Type A, I've been that way all my life."

Male, age thirty: "Women are more Type A than men, they just know how to honey-coat it."

Male, age thirty-six: "I'm a cardiologist and I see more men with a lot of anger than women. Maybe it's a different type of Type A."

Male, age thirty-five: "I think men are brought up to be more competitive. It's changing but still holds true."

Female, age twenty-three: "Not that we're less aggressive, but we're taught to be less aggressive. A majority of my friends aren't pushovers, but they'd be more likely to back down than the guys."

Female, age twenty-two: "Women were always Type A's, they just didn't act on it."

The Truth

When we think of the Type A personality (competitive, impatient, achieving, time pressured, and often angry), most of us think of a man in a business suit. Though some of the qualities of this personality aren't especially desirable—the anger in particular is associated with an increased risk of heart disease—we also think of them as somewhat necessary for survival. And without the hostile component, we may even think of Type A behavior as "all-American" ambition and drive!

Because women weren't as large a part of the workforce when the Type A research was first done in the early seventies, we have reached the backwards conclusion that women aren't success-oriented or achievement-driven people. We assumed their nurturing capacity made them more suitable to raising children, rather than seeing their nurturing as one of *many* capacities.

The truth is that women are as motivated to achieve as men:

—We can be success-driven, just like men—trying to be the perfect lover, mother, daughter, friend, and employee.

—We can be in a hurry, just like men—impatient when our child is slow to dress, a subordinate asks questions about an assignment, our mate talks about something that doesn't interest us.

—We can be irritable, just like men—and call it constructive criticism.

—We can be aggressive rather than assertive, just like men.

—We can compete just like men and get a great kick out of winning.

But unlike most men who are Type A's, we also tend to give others enormous power to affect our feelings about ourselves through their reactions to us.

And we can try to do too much, either because we enjoy approval or because we're more practiced at playing "catch-up" than at playing for fun.

For better and worse, then, women, like men, are frequently Type A:

↦ ***Most women are Type A.*** For the past two decades, the Stress Program that I direct at Mount Sinai School of Medicine in New York City has been collecting data on the Type A woman, and many of these data were reported in my earlier books *The Female Stress Syndrome* and *Quick Fixes & Small Comforts.* We have asked more than 6,000 women to rate themselves on the following scale and, in fact, have *rarely* found a woman who *didn't* have Type A behaviors.

FEMALE TYPE A BEHAVIOR QUIZ

Rate the following statements using these numbers:

0 = never true for you
1 = occasionally true
2 = usually true

_____ I am exacting, even when I don't want to be.
_____ I am always thinking about how much I have to do and how much others are slowing me down.
_____ I end up doing most things myself.
_____ I prefer being busy to being bored, because I like adrenaline as a stimulant.
_____ I tend to do at least two, maybe three, things at the same time: get dressed while talking business on the phone *and* monitoring the children.
_____ I try to avoid lines, because I hate to wait.

The scoring may surprise you. Even *one point* means you are Type A in some way. And that means you have the advantages that go with high energy and drive. But if your score is above five points, you suffer from the disadvantages as well.

Even though the achievement-driven woman may actually enjoy the rush of adrenaline she gets from stress, like any stimulant adrenaline can lead to symptoms such as fatigue, shortness of breath, trouble falling asleep or staying asleep, headaches, weight gain or loss, and palpitations.

↔ ***As doctors have told men for decades, Type A behavior isn't good for health:***

—Heart disease. The hostility of Type A behavior may increase heart disease for both men and women, says Redford B. Williams, M.D., director of the Behavioral Medicine Research Center at Duke University in Durham, North Carolina, and author with Virginia Williams, Ph.D., of *Anger Kills*. The result can be high blood pressure and damage to the arteries.

—High cholesterol. Cholesterol goes up with stress. When people at the University of Pittsburgh School of Medicine tried to solve a confusing puzzle, for example, their cholesterol went up four points.

—Colds. Under extreme stress, we're at least twice as likely to catch a cold, conclude a number of studies. The people in this study had just moved, changed jobs, or been divorced.

—Skin troubles. Skin is a good mirror of stress. Stress can make us blush, turn pale, or actually break out in hives, itching, eczema, acne, or psoriasis.

—Weight gain. In times of stress, food can be a great source of comfort! But being overweight isn't healthy: Studies show that many extra pounds can put us at greater risk of heart disease, diabetes, backache, varicose veins, and high blood pressure.

—Other effects. And then there are the "minor" effects of job-related stress in women I see in my practice: the pounding migraine headaches, the searing heartburn, the anorexia and bulimia, the depression, the anxiety. In his book *Treating Type A Behavior—and Your Heart*, cardiologist Meyer Friedman, M.D., the first to identify Type A behavior, also says that Type A women sigh, click their tongues, and grind their teeth more than Type A men.

How can stress do all this? Its main action is to prepare us for short-term, immediate danger. Stress causes the brain to signal glands to release a flood of hormones. These carry messages throughout the body, signaling blood vessels to constrict, the muscles to tense, the immune system to go on hold, and blood fats to rise. This fight-or-flight response may have helped our ancestors gear up and either get away from danger or fight it off. But in today's civilized world, we can't lash out with our fists or run away. So if the fight-or-flight response goes on and on, the unused hormones circulate in the bloodstream, damaging organs and systems.

How to Use the Truth

The choice is clear: Become more aware of when your Type A behavior starts to hurt you rather than help you, and try to practice modification. Start by modifying your thinking. Thinking is a behavior you can change and control:

—Think about what you *can* do rather than what you *should* do.

—Think about delegating responsibility more and personalizing others' behavior less.

—Think less about future fantasies or past glories and more about shaping today.

—Think about the humor in daily life and laugh out loud.

Next, learn to pause and de-stress, because relieving stress can save your life! Here are ten ways to start:

1. Manage anger. It's not true that Type A behavior *in general* is linked to heart attacks, but since one Type A component, anger, *can* be dangerous, it's vital we understand how anger can threaten us and how we can manage it.

First, let's review anger surges. For two decades, research has reported that anger is related to an increased risk of heart attack. A very recent study confirms this once again. A Harvard Medical School team of scientists led by Murray A. Mittleman, M.D., evaluated the anger levels of more than 1,600 women and men who'd had heart attacks in the past and found the average risk of another heart attack increased 2.3 times after intense anger—and the danger lasts for approximately two hours! The American Heart Association explains that this is because anger can increase blood pressure and cause arteries to narrow immediately. Long-term, chronic anger also means increases in blood cholesterol and heart rates, and a decrease in immunity.

Now let's talk about suppressing anger. It can be an even greater risk to a woman's health than angry outbursts! Unlike male heart attack survivors who are at greatest risk if they're explosive, a study at Rush Presbyterian–St. Luke's Medical Center in Chicago finds female heart-attack survivors who "put a lid on their anger" are more likely to suffer fatal heart problems . . . probably because the anger goes on and on and undermines a sense of control over one's emotional life. In 1993 a study at the University of Tennessee in Knoxville found that women who scored high on hostility but low on expression (meaning they were "quick-tempered" but didn't want anyone to know it) had higher blood-pressure readings than women who were able to "let it out." And the famous Framingham Heart Study found women who reported suppressing their anger experienced the highest rate of first heart attacks.

Not that I'm recommending we "let it all hang out." Every angry explosion makes everyone around us either defensive or angry and gives them permission to vent their anger, too. The real message here is that *both* explosive anger *and* suppressed anger create problems, so managing and moderating anger is the answer:

—Count to ten. Then if you have to, count to ten again. Grandma said it works, and it does. It gives you a chance to decide on an active, *not reactive,* response when you're angry. It allows the adrenaline level to drop a bit, so you can think more clearly. And it gives you a sense of control again, just when you probably need it most. It also gives those around you a lesson in what you expect them to do when they're enraged.

—Don't take the bait. If you're being provoked, find a sensible answer, such as "I hear you," and repeat it again and again until your tormentor gives up.

—Write it out. When your rage is overwhelming and you don't trust yourself to manage your anger face-to-face, try writing out your anger. Get it all out on paper and put it away for a day. Then review it more objectively. Rewrite until you're satisfied that every feeling was described accurately. Now put it away again. Then, on the second re-read, decide what you will and will not actually say. By then you'll probably be much more objective and know that letters can be discarded more easily than relationships.

And from the authors of *Type A Behavior and Your Heart*: "If you are overly hostile, certainly the most important drill measure you should adopt is that one in which you remind yourself of the fact that you are hostile. Being forewarned, you are far less inclined to flare up at any stimulus short of one that would induce hostility in anybody."

2. Slow down. Type A time pressure and "hurry sickness" set us up for short tempers and irritability, and two-thirds of all Americans feel they're always rushed, according to Day-Timers, Inc. As one mother told the researchers, "When I have any spare time, I go to the bathroom!" So schedule in as many breaks for yourself as you can during the day, and if you think you don't have time for them, remember how much time-out you'll have if you become ill.

3. Don't isolate yourself. Friends can save your life. They can lend a hand, give you tips, tell you when you sound too harried, confront you when you're becoming aggressive instead of assertive, give you an opportunity to complain or compare yourself to someone less fortunate, or to laugh . . . especially to laugh.

4. Conserve adrenaline. The adrenaline we produce when we're pressured is a natural stimulant, and like all stimulants, it suppresses appetite and energizes. But, remember, as with all stimulants, too much adrenaline begins to disturb sleep, make us irritable, and give us headaches. And withdrawal can do the same thing, so we feel out of sorts on Sundays and restless on vacations, and can't sit still during a movie. The answer is to use adrenaline moderately, get enough sleep so the level will drop during the night, and set priorities so you can drop items from your "to do" list when the day becomes overscheduled.

5. Practice de-stressing. In a study of 1,012 post–heart attack subjects, Dr. Friedman found that those who had practiced de-stressing behavior-modification drills had fewer recurrences of heart attacks than those who watched their diet and exercised but did not modify their Type A behavior. So try these drills:

    —Do one thing at a time at least one hour a day. Concentrate on one activity only—reading, eating, or speaking on the phone—so the adrenaline level needed for simultaneous activity can decrease.

    —Every time you perceive signs of annoyance, tension, or fatigue, de-stress on the spot, not days or hours later. *On the spot.* The classic exercise for this is described by Herbert Benson, M.D., in *The Relaxation Response*:

- *Sit quietly in a comfortable position.*
- *Close your eyes.*
- *Deeply relax all your muscles,* beginning at your feet and progressing up to your face. Keep them relaxed.
- *Become aware of your breathing.* The rhythm lulls stress because no vigilance is needed. The brain knows exactly what's coming next. Then count as you breathe. For example, breathe in . . . out, "One"; breathe in . . . out, "Two"; etc. Breathe easily and naturally.

—Continue for ten to twenty minutes. You may open your eyes to check the time, but don't use an alarm. When you finish, sit quietly for several minutes, at first with your eyes closed and later with your eyes open. Don't stand up for a few minutes.

—Don't worry about whether you're successful in achieving a deep level of relaxation. Maintain a passive attitude and permit relaxation to occur at its own pace. When distracting thoughts occur, try to ignore them by not dwelling upon them and return to your breathing exercise. With practice, the response should come with little effort. Practice the technique once or twice daily, but not within two hours after any meal, since the digestive process seems to interfere with the elicitation of the relaxation response.

—Morning and evening, when you're in bed, try the drill called *progressive muscle relaxation:* You start with the toes and end with the face. First tense your toes—tighten the muscles there until the toes curl. Now relax them. Enjoy the relaxed feeling for a moment before you move on to your calf muscles. And so on. You may find that some muscle groups are already tense and don't need much extra tightening before you try to relax them—the shoulders and neck often are tight all the time.

6. Keep lists. High-energy women need lists. A list gives us a sense of control and organization, relieves our memory of overload, and gives us a chance to prioritize. And besides, crossing something off the list after it's done is one of life's great satisfactions. (Number One on the list should be the thing that will cause the most stress tomorrow if it is left undone today!)

7. Get real. Many of us were raised to be good girls, and now we want to be excellent women. But we can't do it all, have it all, be it all, simultaneously. As the kids say, get real. Pick and choose how you spend your time and energy. When your efforts aren't appreciated, save your time and energy. When your efforts aren't any use, save your time and energy.

8. Get the family to help out. If you're a woman with a family, you're probably doing more than your share of the dirty work. Since nagging doesn't work, here are some plans for rescuing yourself from the dirty work:

—First, target yourself. No one will pitch in if they know you'll do the work eventually, so drop the extras.

—Next, target your mate and negotiate. Being practical is the key. List all the essential tasks from buying groceries to taking out the garbage. Score them for frequency and difficulty. For example, vacuuming is daily but easy, mending is harder but infrequent.

—Then divide tasks up. Let each family member claim the chore he or she wants, then split the rest fairly, put the schedule on paper, and post it. If everyone has a sense of choice, it usually works.

—And now, target your children. Decide what you can tolerate and what you won't tolerate, and then trade off. Refuse a service until a chore is done. No laundry until the bed is made, or no new clothes until hangers are used. Child psychologists warn that children will say they don't care at first but usually come around. Or trade services. You'll clean their room if they clean the bathtubs or do the marketing.

9. Take a mental mini-vacation. Imagining a peaceful place can actually lower blood pressure, relax muscles, and make the brain produce the slow, smooth waves called alpha waves. So find some images that relax you: perhaps being in a private place you knew as a child, looking at the water, looking at the stars. Dr. Herbert Benson speculates that there are probably some two to three thousand research papers linking stress and illness, so start the imagery, yoga, meditation, or exercise now.

10. But don't slow down too much. I remember sociologist Pepper Schwartz of the University of Washington in Seattle saying during a panel discussion for *Woman* magazine, "Blessed are the stressed." She explained that women who do many activities and have many roles have the best mental health and marriage stability because their self-esteem is high, one area of their life can compensate for others, they judge themselves more broadly, and of course they're never bored. Our research at Mount Sinai's Stress Program finds, however, that all this is true only when women have some sense of choice about their activities. So don't let your success-oriented and achievement-driven behaviors take on a life of their own.

I advise my patients, students, and readers to turn their palms up and look at the lifeline. It has a beginning, a middle, and an end. It does not go on forever. Be reminded that life does not go on forever, either. The time to change behavior is now.

COUNTERING THE MYTH OF COMPLACENCY

Women are entitled to all their feelings, and that includes competitiveness, drive, and a desire for success. Women are also entitled to vacations, private time, and other rewards. So:

Prioritize. You can enjoy adrenaline highs without the whole Type A package. Give up that hostility, impatience, and hurrying that are threatening your life, and keep the enthusiasm and energy.

Depressurize. Though achievements can bring great satisfaction, don't measure your success by how many people besides you recognize your accomplishments.

Internalize. Take to heart what you know about moderating your Type A behavior. Practice makes perfect . . . but who says we have to be perfect?

CHAPTER 4

The Myth:

"Women are not as sexual as men"

The Myth:

- Women would rather shop or sleep than make love.
- Women act interested in sex for their partner's sake.
- Women usually fake orgasm.
- Women prefer cuddling to sex.
- Women usually disapprove of oral sex.
- Women don't masturbate.
- Sexual arousal takes much longer for a woman than a man.
- Older women would rather not be bothered.
- Younger women prefer less frequent sex than younger men.
- Women lose interest in sex by midlife.
- Women prefer men to initiate sex.

Who Believes It?

You might not be surprised to learn that, according to our PRODIGY Poll, most of the men and women buying into this myth are married and over forty-five years old! But the way it breaks down for men and women separately does have some surprises.

Among men, one in four married men, one in five divorced men, but only one in six single men thinks women are not very interested in sex.

In occupation categories, one in three male machinists and laborers believes the myth, but only one in five men in sales, clerical positions, and service occupations does. This may reflect either the daily contact with women customers and coworkers for men in sales (which gives them an opportunity to hear women talk), or perhaps the biases of the men who are more likely to choose employment as laborers, machinists, or handlers.

Among women in these same occupations, it's a very different picture:

Women machinists, laborers, and handlers are the *least* likely to think women are not interested in sex. Ninety-one percent said the statement is *not true*, and none of them said they were "unsure."

Widows, on the other hand, were the most likely of the female respondents to have answered "unsure" to the statement about women and sex (15 percent). Divorced women were not unsure at all. In fact, 90 percent of divorced or separated women said it's not true that women were less interested in sex than men.

In general, only 9 percent of women said they think women have low sexual interest, compared to almost 25 percent of all men in the poll. And although nearly three quarters of all our survey participants—73 percent—reject the notion that women aren't that interested in sex, women are more certain than men: 85 percent of the women and 67 percent of the men say it's not so.

Our interviews with the non-computer-based local surveys confirmed the PRODIGY Poll trend:

Eighty-eight percent of the women but only 50 percent of the men said women are not less interested in sex than men. And they added this information: Both women (68 percent) and men (92 percent) said they thought more men than women are interested in sex after age sixty. But 60 percent of the women (and 48 percent of the men) said women make love with more *passion* than men.

Here are some comments from survey participants:

Female, age twenty-four: "Women hold themselves back sexually so they don't overwhelm guys."

Female, age forty-two: "Women are much more sexual than men because we're sensual, too."

Male, age fifty-seven: "Women are kidding themselves if they think men can stop thinking about sex all the time."

Male, age thirty-four: "I think women want sex to prove the man's love to her, not because it's fun."

Male, age sixty-eight: "Women are always talking about what men are 'really like' sexually. I've never heard a man talk about what women are 'really like' sexually. Men talk to men, so we know we're sexual. I don't know about women. Do women talk to women?"

Female, age forty-five: "Men think having an orgasm is having sex. That's the difference."

The Truth

If it seems as if men are more interested in sex than women are, it's probably because surveys find women want more than sex—women want intimacy, too. While men seem to focus on the pleasure of orgasm, women want that and affection, too. In *The Janus Report on Sexual Behavior*, 34 percent of women strongly agree that sex and intimacy are two different things; only 21 percent of men strongly agree.

↝ *Women feel sensual.*

—A majority of Americans (75 percent) think that women are more sensual than men, according to a survey commissioned by Revlon. Only 8 percent felt men are more sensual, and 13 percent thought the sexes are equally sensual. And according to *The Janus Report*, 85 percent of women feel that sex is "deliciously sensual" or close to it.

⊷ *Women of all ages are sexual.*

—More news from *The Janus Report*. Nearly half (46 percent) of women ages eighteen through twenty-six are sexually active—they have sex daily or a few times weekly. The same is true for 49 percent of women twenty-seven through thirty-eight, 39 percent of women thirty-nine through fifty, 32 percent of women fifty-one through sixty-four, and 41 percent of women sixty-five and over.

—According to *The Starr and Weiner Report on Sex and Sexuality in the Mature Years*, three of every four elderly women who are sexually active say their lovemaking has improved. The report by Bernard Starr, a psychology professor, and M. E. Weiner, a gerontologist and psychologist, contains the results of interviews with nearly 1,000 elderly men and women.

—One of every six women will be more interested in sex as she ages, according to research at the Duke University Center for the Study of Aging. The center also finds that 80 percent of couples in their seventies are still interested in sex, and 70 percent of them are having sex about once a week. So much for women losing interest after midlife!

In fact, the only physical change that may interfere with sexual spontaneity for women is some vaginal dryness, which can be easily managed with a vaginal lubricant, moisturizer, or prescribed estrogen-replacement therapy. Part of the myth of sexlessness in older women may come from the fact that a woman's partner has died. Without partners, some women suppress their libido, and the myth that older women are not interested in sex is perpetuated.

⊷ *Women are frequently sexual.* A recent book by sociologist Edward Laumann, *The Social Organization of Sexuality*, tells us that in general:

—Men and women report the same frequency of sex.

—Thirty percent of men and 26 percent of women have sex two to three times a week.

—Thirty-six percent of men and 37 percent of women have sex a few times a month.

—Twenty-seven percent of men and 30 percent of women have sex a few times a year.

And the 1994 *Parade* magazine "Sex in America" survey tells us that women, like men, would like to have sex twice as often as they do now. But among live-in lovers, the same report finds that women have more sex than men. Forty-three percent of the women compared to 37 percent of the men in this category reported having sex two or three times a week.

↔ ***Women have orgasms.***

—More than 50 percent of women frequently have orgasm during sex, according to *The Janus Report*. And aging itself seems to have no effect on a woman's capacity for orgasm—although illness, medication, pain, over-the-counter drugs, loss of a partner, and stress may interfere. Even a woman's capacity for multiple orgasms is undiminished, and as we explained in Chapter 2, some women find that as their estrogen levels drop off, their drive to orgasm actually increases.

↔ ***Women want more than cuddling.*** As for the popular notion that women prefer "just cuddling," the National Health and Social Life Survey reported in *Sex in America* tells us:

—Ninety-two percent of women have orgasms with their primary partner; 71 percent say "usually" or "always."

—Seventy-eight percent of women find vaginal intercourse "very appealing."

—Seventy-one percent of women spent at least fifteen minutes to an hour making love during their most recent experience.

—Sixty-seven percent of women said they like to initiate sex (compared to 54 percent of men), according to a survey for *Redbook* magazine.

↔ ***Most women masturbate.*** *The Janus Report* tells us:

—Only 12 percent of married women have never masturbated (6 percent of married men), and

—An equal percentage of women and men agree that masturbation is a natural part of life and continues on in marriage (67 percent of women, 66 percent of men).

↔ ***Women take men to sex therapy.*** A few years ago a survey I directed, while supervisor of the Human Sexuality Program at Mt. Sinai School of Medicine, found that in seventeen sex therapy clinics associated with teaching universities, it was women more frequently than men who were bringing partners for co-counseling. The rates of premature ejaculation and erectile dysfunction were higher among admissions than lack of sexual desire or lack of orgasm in women.

↪ ***Women are open about sex.*** The *Parade* magazine survey found:

—Seventy percent of women feel comfortable talking about sex, an increase of 11 percent since a decade ago, and *The Janus Report* tells us an equal percentage of women and men consider oral sex to be normal or acceptable (87 percent of women, 88 percent of men).

↪ ***Women don't really "take longer."*** Last but not least, a report by Anne Moir and David Jessel in *Brain Sex* tells us women don't take longer than men to become aroused, as is widely believed. Researchers say it takes just seconds for vaginal lubrication to start. But women may be *turned off* more easily than men during early stages of arousal unless they are touched gently.

How to Use the Truth

The secret of a successful and safer sex life is knowledge, particularly for women. Knowledge helps us understand ourselves sexually. It turns confusion into curiosity and stops myths from becoming self-fulfilling prophecies. It helps us understand our sexual past. It helps us prepare for our sexual future and protect our health, and frankly, it's filled with good news. Those of us who have bought into the myth of female asexuality can also buy out of it! Here's how we can develop sexual potential if we choose.

↪ ***Start with sensuality.*** Men are learning something women have known for a long time: If a couple starts with sensuality, they usually end up with sex too. So touch, hug, kiss hello, hold hands in the movies, massage each other's back as you watch television, brush each other's hair, pass the soap in the shower, and wash each other. No demands, no plans. Don't think of it as foreplay, just fun. Create the opportunity and sex will happen. *And when it does, protect yourself and your partner from all sexually transmitted diseases.*

↪ ***Talk together.*** I recommend a ten-minute "bare minimum" at night. That means hand-in-hand, face-to-face talk. The 1994 *Parade* survey found that three out of four men (74 percent) now say it's easy to talk about sex—what feels good, what feels bad. About 70 percent of women say the same. This is important news for both sexes: A line of communication we thought was closed has actually been open; now we know it's there to use.

The "conversation" is important. It's natural to assume that other people like the same things we do, but that's far from the truth when it comes to sex. Although both the male and female orgasms involve rhythmic contractions of the same genital muscles, and in both sexes the contractions occur at the rate of 0.9 per second (each one takes just a bit longer than one second), there are person-to-person variations in preferences, pleasure spots, pain thresholds, and physical endurance. Now we can talk about them.

A decade of sex therapy tells us that the more we share requests, the more pleasure our partner will be able to give us and the more comfortable he or she will feel making requests, too. So don't be afraid to ask your mate: What's your favorite time to make love? In the sun or at night? Where? What turns you on the most? What turns you off? Do you like it when I do this? And don't be afraid to let your partner know what you're enjoying while you're enjoying it!

There's only one wall that should probably stay up: Think twice—even three times—before you tell your partner about fantasies featuring other people. Even if your mate is "one of many" in your life (past or present), let your lover be your one and only for this moment. Your lover may forgive your fantasies but will probably never forget them. It's a high price to pay for momentary arousal.

↠ *Don't buy into boredom.* Marriage doesn't mean the end of sex. In fact, live-in lovers and married couples have sex more often than singles who are dating! And studies show that although sexual activity may dip during those difficult child-rearing years, once the nest begins to empty, sexual interest surges. According to *The Janus Report*, the age at which men have sex most often isn't their twenties, thirties, or forties—it's their fifties. And women sixty-five and over are as active as women in their twenties! It's easier during these periods of our lives to relax and play in bed, to focus on feelings and sensations, to forget the past and future and just be together.

↠ *Expect emotional involvement.* Men and women are becoming more equally interested in intimacy. According to the *Parade* magazine survey, in 1984, 86 percent of women were looking for an emotional attachment to their partner, and as of 1994 the same percentage

still do. But men were a different story. In 1984, only 59 percent were looking for an emotional attachment. But now 71 percent of men say they find it difficult to have sex unless there's an emotional connection. This means a woman who still believes that a man wants only sex—and therefore closes herself emotionally—could be denying *him* a connection he wants and needs. This also means you can help a partner who's not interested by removing all pressure to have sex and replacing it with acts of affection. Spend more time together in nonsexual activities that both of you enjoy. The result, in time, could be an exchange of feelings that is true lovemaking.

↔ ***Try morning sex.*** Most of us make love at night, even though we know it may not be the best time. We tend to be stressed, exhausted, distracted, worried about children staying in bed, or full from dinner or snacks. Experts recommend that we consider making love in the morning because we're rested, daily life hasn't intruded yet, our body temperature climbs in the morning and makes us feel relaxed, and men often experience morning arousal, which we can use to our advantage. (By the way, that arousal has to do with the sleep cycle and hormonal patterns, not full bladders.) Women say they like the closeness they feel after spending the night with bodies touching. So you may want to put some breath spray next to the bed, set the alarm a bit earlier tomorrow or send the children to their grandparents this weekend, and try some morning love.

↔ ***Give yourself permission.*** If our mothers, fathers, or husbands will not grant us permission to be sexual, we can grant ourselves that permission. Women of all ages are sexual and can be comfortable with that fact. Comfort can lead to relaxation and guilt-free pleasure, which mean a fuller sex life, more frequent orgasms, and a better relationship with a mate. Sometimes realizing that it's normal to be sexual is enough to release a woman's sexual responses. But sometimes it's not. If you find that your arousal is infrequent or inhibited, orgasm is difficult, intercourse is uncomfortable, or your satisfaction is low, please consider sex therapy alone or with your mate.

↔ ***Think of the benefits.*** Passion can give us a cardiovascular workout comparable to that from light jogging, can reduce stress symptoms by stimulating the body to produce a natural tranquilizer called oxytocin, and there's even evidence that sexual arousal can ease the

pain of arthritis and some allergies by increasing our production of cortisol. Sex also stimulates neurotransmitters that act as natural antidepressants, analgesics, and stimulants; helps prevent migraines; renews intimacy; expresses love—and is neither fattening nor expensive! So lovemaking not only feels good, safe sex can be good for you, too.

↪ ***Make a date.*** The real enemy of lovemaking isn't the passage of time, it's the lack of time. So make yourself make time. After all, we plan for meals, work, dental visits, errands, and television programs. When we're single we set aside time for meeting men, and when we're married we set aside time for dinner guests. Now set aside time for pleasure.

Time is particularly important for women because our definition of great sex is usually not instant physical arousal, overpowering fantasies, or a rush to end the experience. We usually want more than an orgasm. We want lovemaking, and that takes some lingering, laughing, and luscious sensuality. How do sex and lovemaking differ? Sex is driven by the heat of passion; but lovemaking creates the heat of passion. It doesn't rush toward orgasm; lovemaking reluctantly ends with orgasm. Lovemaking takes time: to learn and to linger. Lovemaking is not for leftover time. Practice making time and taking time for pleasure.

↪ ***Ask for what you need.*** Whether it's nature or nurture, men and women are often sexually different. Remember, even though it's natural to pleasure our partner the way we'd like to be pleasured, it doesn't always work out. So make requests. Not demands, orders, or dissertations, just requests. Requests are flattering because you're putting yourself in a partner's hands, and considerate because your partner doesn't have to try to read your mind. Besides, you're giving your mate implicit permission to make requests, too.

↪ ***Have a menopause check.*** The average age of menopause in the United States is 50.8 years of age, but many women begin to feel changes (vaginal dryness, hot flashes, cold sweats, mood swings) long before menopause. Not very conducive to sexual fantasies! And many women who have had surgical removal of the ovaries find that the difference in desire can be quite sudden. If this sounds familiar, see a gynecologist. As we mentioned briefly in Chapter 2 (on midlife), there

are many ways to manage menopausal symptoms. About 30 percent of women in menopause are on hormone replacement therapy (HRT). And many gynecologists find that when hot flashes and vaginal dryness are controlled, women's sexual interest is maintained.

↪ ***Have a libido check.*** Many physicians are becoming convinced that the male hormone testosterone plays a major role in a woman's sex drive, too. Women who at age eighteen had four sexual thoughts a day may have one a *week* by age fifty, says Winifred B. Cutler, Ph.D., in her book *Love Cycles.* But you don't have to lose your libido. Menopausal women who no longer have sexual daydreams, have no appetite for sex, and can't get aroused can suspect a lack of testosterone, according to Gloria A. Bachmann, M.D., of the Robert Wood Johnson Medical School in New Brunswick, New Jersey. In a recent experiment at Baylor College of Medicine in Houston, women on estrogen/testosterone therapy had a higher sex drive and made love more often. Some hormone replacement formulas now contain testosterone as well as estrogen and progesterone.

↪ ***See a physician for him.*** If you're worried about your male partner's heart-attack risk, see a physician with him, and if you get a go-ahead to have sex, stop worrying. "Death by orgasm" is extremely unlikely: Fewer than 1 percent of all heart-attack deaths come during sex, according to experts at the National Institute on Aging. And 70 percent of those sex-related deaths are associated with an extramarital partner, not a spouse!

If a male partner is having erection problems, a physician can check out possible physical causes. Blood-pressure or other medication, over-the-counter drugs, illness (diabetes and multiple sclerosis are common causes), vascular conditions, and neurological changes may account for more than 50 percent of all erectile dysfunction. Sex therapy may also help physical problems: in these sessions a man can learn that he can have an orgasm without a full erection, can find out alternatives to intercourse, and can get a fix on how his mate is feeling physically as well as emotionally.

↪ ***Treat depression.*** Depression changes a number of chemical systems in the body, including the neurotransmitters that direct the sex drive. But some medicines for depression can actually lower desire, too, or interfere with the ability to achieve orgasm, probably by altering the balance of the chemicals in the brain; so ask your physician about side effects.

↣ **Check your medication.** Any medication—whether sold over the counter or by prescription only—may cause side effects that can dampen sexual function or pleasure. Taking antihistamines nonstop for more than a week or so, for example, may make arousal difficult because they can reduce secretions, including those of the vagina. As for other medicine, data are scant for women—it's much easier to measure the male response! Philip Luloff, M.D., assistant clinical professor of psychiatry at the Mount Sinai School of Medicine, who has studied the effects of drugs on human sexuality, suspects that the drugs that decrease desire for men do the same for women.

According to Dr. Luloff, medicines that may *delay* orgasm in women include:

thioridazine (Mellaril)

trifluoperazine (Stelazine)

imipramine (Tofranil)

Medicines that may *reduce* orgasm in women include:

anticholinergics

clonidine (Catapres)

methyldopa (Aldomet)

monoamine oxidase inhibitors (MAOIs)

tricyclic antidepressants (TADs)

fluoxetine hydrochloride (Prozac)

paroxetine hydrochloride (Paxil)

sertraline hydrochloride (Zoloft)

And those that may *inhibit* orgasm completely include:

clomipramine (Anafranil)

amoxapine (Asendin)

phenelzine (Nardil)

isocarboxazid (Marplan)

nortriptyline (Aventyl, Pamelor)

If desire, arousal, or orgasm changes soon after a new or different medicine schedule, perhaps a change of dosage, a switch of medicine, or a shift in the time of day it's taken will solve the problem.

↤ *Treat vaginal infections.* Besides being uncomfortable and dangerous, vaginal infections and sexually transmitted diseases can interfere with lubrication, making sex painful. Postmenopausal women are especially susceptible, since the lining of the vagina tends to lose its normal infection-fighting acidity then. Yeast remedies are available over the counter, and a physician can prescribe antibiotics for chlamydia, gonorrhea, and others. It's important to treat vaginal infections and sexually transmitted diseases promptly. Untreated, many can lead to pelvic inflammatory disease, a severe infection of the uterus, fallopian tubes, and ovaries that may even leave a woman infertile.

↤ *Use a lubricant.* Vaginal dryness is a problem for many women. Removal of precancerous cells or small growths from the vaginal wall with a laser can create dryness. So can some types of chemotherapy. So can some medications we've mentioned. And so, of course, can hormonal changes. During menopause, the tissues of the vulva become thinner and lose their engorgement response. The vagina may shrink in size and lose some of its elasticity. After a few episodes of painful intercourse (called dyspareunia), a woman may become so nervous that her muscles tighten and make intercourse even more painful. Giving up on intercourse is usually not the answer, since regular arousal and intercourse increase estrogen levels and vaginal lubrication. Try additional vaginal moisturizers or lubricants to make sex more pleasant. (But avoid petroleum-based products if you're using a condom: hand lotion, baby oil, petroleum jelly, or other petroleum-based lubricants can break down latex and make the condom ineffective as a barrier against AIDS and other diseases.) If pain still persists, see your physician. Think about psychological counseling, too, to help separate the pain from the fear response to the pain.

↤ *Treat illness.* Untreated diabetes can create sexual problems. In women, extra sugar in the blood can change the acidity of the vagina, which may affect lubrication and nerves that carry impulses that trigger the sexual response. Diabetes is easily detectable by a blood test and diet, exercise, or sometimes insulin can be recommended by your physician to bring it under control. Other nerve conditions can short-circuit sexual fulfillment also: Parkinson's disease, multiple sclerosis, a stroke, or spinal cord injuries. Of course, fatigue, headache, dizziness, or any disease that causes them will block enthusiastic sex as well.

↔ ***Prevent illness.*** Women are more at risk for sexually transmitted diseases than heterosexual men because intercourse is internal for us and membranes that line the vagina are more delicate and more likely to become infected than the outer skin of the penis. We can reduce our risk by using latex condoms and a spermicide with nonoxynol-9 (check the labels).

The Kinsey Institute New Report on Sex also suggests:

—delaying sexual intercourse and reducing the number of sexual partners you have in order to lower your exposure to sexually transmitted diseases

—avoiding any unprotected sexual behaviors (all forms of oral, genital, or anal sex) until you are in a mutually monogamous relationship and a *physician* has assured you that neither of you is infected

—arming yourself with information about the transmission of the deadly human immunodeficiency virus (HIV), which can enter the body through microscopically tiny breaks in the mucous membranes of the mouth, anus, or vagina, or in the skin anywhere on the body

—arming yourself with information about other viral infections (herpes, genital warts), as well as bacterial infections (gonorrhea, syphilis, chlamydia, for example), yeast infections (candida albicans, trichomonas vaginalis), and protozoa (pubic lice, scabies)

Again, knowledge is power.

Since physicians now recognize so many more sex problems as physical than they did ten years ago, the best place to begin is with a complete physical exam. This will rule out illnesses that can get in the way of sex. Next stop is a gynecologist, but many are too shy or uninformed to talk over a woman's sex problems with her. So if you have a question, don't hesitate to take the lead. If the physician seems uncomfortable, give him or her a chance. If the doctor still won't deal with your problems, ask for a referral to a sex therapist or a sex clinic.

A fun and fulfilling sex life: it's something already within us, waiting to be released if we choose it.

COUNTERING THE MYTH OF FEMALE SEXLESSNESS

We're born with the capacity for sexuality and remain sexual throughout our lives. If you want to enjoy your sexuality more:

Accept that you are a sexual being and that being sexual is normal.

Understand that you may not always feel sexual, however, and that you are entitled to make each sexual decision separately and deliberately.

Ask for what you need from your partner. (Requests are flattering and permission-giving, and increase your chance of being satisfied.) Insist on safer sex. (For your partner's sake as well as your own.)

Tell the appropriate women in your life about important sexual information. One study I directed recently found that the majority of more than a thousand women said they did *not* discuss sex issues, sex problems, or sex information with friends or female family members. Those "mother-daughter talks" and "sisterly secrets" and pajama party discussions have been more of a myth than the truth. Let's share important information and keep on talking.

CHAPTER 5

The Myth:

*"Vanity,
thy name
is woman"*

The Myth:

- Women are always late because they're primping.
- We look in the mirror whenever we're near one.
- "Bad" hair can ruin our day.
- We start dyeing our hair when the first gray hair appears.
- Breaking a nail is a major tragedy.
- We're never thin enough to please ourselves.
- We obsess about our thighs, breasts, and stomachs.
- We worry that smiling creates wrinkles.

Who Believes It?

Exactly half of all the men in our PRODIGY Poll buy into this one, with divorced or separated men believing it the most.

About one in four women (24 percent) believes this myth, with single women (25 percent) believing it very slightly more than women who are married (23 percent) or divorced or separated (22 percent).

Nearly half of all men and women over forty-five believe that women are vain (49 percent). In the under-forty-five age group, that number drops to just 38 percent.

The non-computer-based local surveys find two out of three women saying they've heard that women are vain and therefore believe flattery more than men do. Two out of three men agreed and think women care more about others' opinion of them than men do. The interviews show about the same male-female split as our PRODIGY Poll:

Female, age twenty-three: "We're not vain . . . just trying to look good for men. Particularly black women, because it's hard for us to find a good mate."

Male, age fifty-four: "Men are equally vain. Everyone worries about how other people see us."

Female, age twenty-one: "When we're very young and very old, I think we care a lot about how others see us. Like when I was a teen, I worried about sweaters and fashion. But in between, who has time for vanity?"

Male, age thirty-five: "Women are probably more vain than men . . . |and| give a little more 'face time' to the mirror."

Female, age forty-eight: "My husband's a plastic surgeon. He says men are as vain as women, but they're not as nit-picking about every detail."

Female, age thirty (hairdresser): "In my salon, guess who looks in the mirror more! Men sneak looks all the time! They think they're gorgeous. Women look at themselves because they don't think they're gorgeous."

The Truth

True vanity—conceit, self-glorification, and total involvement with our image to the exclusion of almost everything else—is unusual. Someone who is so obsessive-compulsive and narcissistic as to fit this definition of "vain" is also likely to have other relationship and job problems that probably require treatment.

We're discussing the kind of vanity that slows us down when we pass a mirror, but doesn't stop us dead in our tracks. And the truth is that both men *and* women are concerned about the way they look. In fact, men sometimes out-preen women.

↦ ***Men like the mirror.*** Men prefer to talk about themselves and are obsessed with going bald, according to a survey of hairdressers attending the 1995 International Beauty Show in New York City. They also stare into the mirror an average of three times longer than women, according to a survey of hundreds of hairstylists reported by Associated Newspapers Ltd. in 1993.

↦ ***Men talk about themselves.*** In fact, that study reports that eight out of ten men made themselves the main topic of conversation during a haircut, compared to only two out of ten women.

↦ ***Men use hair dye, too.*** Women dye their hair only 5 percent more, reported the same hairdressers' study.

↦ ***Men worry about baldness.*** In 1992, 1,955 men had hair plugs, scalp reduction, scalp flaps, or other treatments to fill in bald spots, according to American Society of Plastic and Reconstructive Surgeons (ASPRS) figures.

↦ ***Men love clothes.*** A Scottish study found that in the days before a vacation, 68 percent of men go shopping for clothes, compared to 65 percent of women.

↦ ***Men have augmentation, too.*** More and more men are having penile augmentation, which some experts say is dangerous, reports *USA Today*.

↦ ***Men pump iron.*** One psychiatrist calls it the "Chippendale syndrome"—men addicted to dieting or bulking up and weight-lifting to get those perfect bodies male dancers display at Chippendale's. One million men are estimated to have anorexia or bulimia, and 250,000 teenage boys use steroids to build muscle.

↦ ***Men buy makeup.*** According to the International Beauty Show organization, men spend over $2 billion a year on cosmetics, from skin tanners to blemish concealers.

↦ ***Men want to look like models.*** A survey of male MBA students at Stanford University found nearly all said the role models for their appearance are male models in magazines!

And a *Psychology Today* magazine study a few years ago found 34 percent of male respondents were "dissatisfied with their looks." That was double the number who were dissatisfied a decade earlier.

Why this change in male vanity? Many trend-watchers speculate that it's because the huge number of male baby boomers had to compete with each other for jobs and promotions. And now that they're aging, they also have to compete with younger men . . . and with more women, too. They're learning what social psychologists have always reported: The best jobs usually go to the best-looking candidates because attractive qualities are assumed to go with an attractive appearance.

Now let's talk about women. We seem to be turning more of our efforts toward health rather than appearance. Perhaps this is because our own economic gains mean that "capturing" a rich husband with our beauty is no longer the only key to social success and financial security. Or perhaps it's because we're filling so many roles that we know we have to prime ourselves to last for the long run. We still consume $40 billion worth of cosmetics a year, but most surveys now find women saying they use the cosmetics to please themselves . . . to look healthy when they see their reflection in a window, and to smile when they catch a glimpse of themselves in the mirror.

↪ ***We are not obsessed with our appearance.*** Yes, baby boomers say they'd like to stop the acne now they are twenty years beyond the teen years. And teens don't want acne either. And plastic surgery, liposuction, teeth laminates, and push-up bras sell. But remember, the bottom line is that almost 90 percent of women are basically *not* dissatisfied with their appearance, according to the Replens Report we mentioned in Chapter 1. That's just 4 percentage points away from men (93 percent are satisfied with their appearance).

↪ ***We are not obsessed with our weight.*** Yes, we'd like to be slim enough to buy and wear the clothes we love without wondering how many pairs of control-top stockings we'll have to wear at the same time. But the same study that found we're not obsessed with our appearance also found we're not particularly obsessed with our weight, either. Nearly three quarters (72 percent) of more than 1,000 women surveyed said they are generally content with their bodies, and the same percentage said they're satisfied with their physical fitness, too.

In fact, almost 30 percent of that group said they're *very* satisfied with their physical fitness!

↦ ***Women exercise more for health than vanity.*** A survey of 10,000 households by the National Sporting Goods Association found women outnumber men as frequent participants in the healthful body-toning exercises (not body-building or body-shaping exercises) like walking and swimming—and they're more likely to stick with it than men.

↦ ***Women have mixed feelings about makeup.*** Although about 70 percent of all women use some makeup, even if it's just lipstick, we are not addicted to it. A Yankelovich survey reports that almost half of all women surveyed said they'd feel no different if they woke up tomorrow in a world without cosmetics . . . and almost 15 percent said they'd feel *overjoyed.*

It's also important to note that the survey found that almost 65 percent of the women said they feel attractive without any cosmetics at all!

↦ ***Men have plastic surgery.*** One out of every seven plastic surgery patients is a man.

↦ ***Men have breast surgery.*** In 1992, according to the ASPRS, 4,997 men had breast-reduction operations; 39,639 women had breast reductions.

↦ ***Men have ear surgery.*** ASPRS figures indicate that in 1992 men had 3,058 ear-surgery operations to bring prominent ears closer to the head or to reduce the size of large ears. Women had 3,313 ear operations.

How to Use the Truth

The average woman will spend more than 4,000 hours of her life putting on and touching up makeup, and 200 hours just plucking her eyebrows, reported *Health* magazine several years ago. What do those hours say about us? Some may say that we are perfectionists or feel a deep need to alter the basic equipment we came with; the truth is probably that we simply care about our appearance, want to be well groomed, or are using ourselves as an art canvas. The goal is to find the balance between enhancing ourselves and enjoying ourselves.

↦ *Manage makeup.* If we're so confident about our appearance, why are we using makeup at all? The oldest tradition of makeup is its use to suggest sexual arousal and youth (with its implications that we are fertile and would make good mates who have many childbearing years left). Ethologist Desmond Morris, author of *Intimate Behavior*, writes that rosy cheeks tell the world we are well rested, healthy, and physically active—or perhaps blushing from secret sexual fantasies. Red lips look as though arousal has pushed our blood pressure up and we're ready to be kissed. Eyeliner gives us the wide-eyed look of youth and also makes the pupil look dilated, as it is during sexual excitement. Moisturizer and foundation give the skin a glow akin to the afterglow of lovemaking.

But most women deal with their appearance as matter-of-factly as if they were brushing their teeth. They use some makeup because they know that the face they show the world is important, and because first impressions count!

But if you can't seem to get past the mirror, take control:

—Use the mirror to relax. Women see their reflections an average of seventeen times a day. Don't just check your hair, makeup, and clothes; check your jaw, your brows, and your shoulders. Make each once-over a signal to pause, relax, and breathe—and the resulting calm can improve our appearances better than any makeup or hair-color job.

—Use desensitization techniques. Each week choose one cosmetic to leave out of your regimen. Test reactions. You may get none . . . which will give you more of a sense of choice about using it!

—Use the term "good enough" frequently while you put on your makeup. "Perfect" is impossible.

—Keep saying, "This is fun," as you apply makeup so you won't confuse the procedure with brain surgery.

↦ *Recognize hair-anoia.* Many women seem to have a special relationship with their hair. When we need a change, we change our hairstyle or hair color. When a haircut is bad, we can cry. When a haircut is different, we may barely recognize ourselves in the mirror. If this sounds familiar, don't label yourself vain. Realize that hair is our most easily altered part of the body and the only fashion accessory besides our nails that grows from the body. We use our hair as a quick fix because a haircut is fast, unlike a ten- to twenty-week fitness program, and it's reversible, unlike a nose job.

Hair is also our most visible trademark and statement. If hair is drab, dry, oily, frizzy, uncut, uncombed, or not acceptable to us for any of a million other reasons no one else would notice, we may feel an urge to cancel appointments and spend a quiet day cleaning closets at home.

If you feel too involved with your hair, try keeping a record of the time and money spent on it for a month. If the total is comparable to a hobby and there is time and money in the budget for it, fine. If the total is too high, you're now more aware of your hair-anoia and can start to fight this minor ailment. The record can also indicate whether attacks of hair-anoia coincide with other upsetting events. If you get most crazed about your hair when you're tired or lonely, for example, try to take care of the real problem—by getting some sleep or setting up more visits with friends.

↦ *Set reasonable standards for your body.* Some of us were born with a model's lean body; some of us seem to put on a pound just looking at a doughnut. Researchers have found that body size is ruled partly by genes, so many of us are fighting a losing battle trying to control our weight too tightly. And we may be making ourselves feel worse in two ways:

—We may never reach our weight goal or will be there for only a fleeting moment before yo-yo-ing back upward.

—Our obsession with looking thin can increase our risk of eating disorders.

Almost all of us can improve our body size and shape with a good fitness program, but only *to a point.* It's important to separate the dreamgirl fantasy from the stubborn but manageable body we were given to live in. So assess your health, not just your hips. Remember to rest, eat sensibly, exercise, and drink enough fluids. Use the mirror not to reflect faults but to show you who you are. Look at yourself objectively, not critically.

↦ *Don't put yourself down.* Don't attempt to deflect others' criticism by criticizing yourself! Chances are everyone else is too busy worrying about their own imperfections to notice yours anyway. Instead of nicknaming your hips "the Winnebago" or calling your belly "a pudding," be more objective: "I've gained some weight" or "I should start doing crunches to tighten up these muscles." Even in private, focus on your positives—not only the physical ones but also your warmth, skills, common sense, energy, and humor.

↝ ***Try to accept all compliments graciously.*** Find it hard to take compliments? Don't like being the center of attention or scrutiny? Sometimes even suspect the motives of the "admirer"? Relax! The word is out: Someone, for whatever reason, thinks you're looking good today. If someone says, "You're absolutely radiant," don't answer that it must be the blusher you put on. Enjoy being radiant; who cares about the motive for the compliment? Maybe you really are radiant. A simple "Thank you" is fine. Even better: "I'm happy to hear it" or "Great!"

↝ ***Find people who make you comfortable.*** We aren't always the ones who are most obsessed with our own appearance. Sometimes the pressure comes from people who look at us—a boyfriend, girlfriend, spouse, coworker, or parent. If we appreciate the reminders to eat less, fuss more, or dress better, then we have no conflict. If, however, we are irritated that our critics don't seem to see us beyond our face and body, we may need to enlighten them, meet them on a different level—or get out of their line of sight.

Our hair, face, and body are part of the whole person, our mixed bag to be improved if we choose, enjoyed, but, finally, accepted.

COUNTERING THE
VANITY MYTH

Remember the days when women always dressed up for parties, and never stepped outside without a full makeup job? Today, anything goes—for men as well as women. Businesses that once were the guardians of traditional attire have instituted a dress-down Friday, and women can create their own look . . . so let's make it the healthy, happy look. After all:

Physical beauty is not . . . as important as physical health.

Physical beauty is not . . . key to friendships or love.

Physical beauty is not . . . essential in any way.

Basic beauty is . . . of course, inside.

CHAPTER 6

The Myth:

"Women are too emotional"

The Myth:

- Women overreact.
- Women's raging hormones make them unfit to hold office.
- Women make decisions with their hearts, men make decisions with their heads.
- Women can't think straight when they're premenstrual.
- Women aren't logical enough to run companies.
- Women are suckers for sob stories.
- Women cry when they're happy.
- Women cry when they're angry.
- Women cry when they're sad.
- Women are always crying.

Who Believes It?

About two out of every three men (65 percent) in our PRODIGY Poll agree with the stereotype that women are more emotional, but just one in three women (34 percent) agree. And the older you are, the more likely you are to buy into this belief.

Looking at men separately, divorced or separated men (66 percent) and married men (65 percent) tend to believe this one a little more than single men (61 percent). But only half as many women believe it: 34 percent of married women and 33 percent of divorced or separated women think we're more emotional.

The non-computer-based local surveys established this stereotype as one that is widely endorsed. The quotes from interviewees on this topic include these:

Female, age eighteen: "My father's always calling me a drama queen, but my brother's always getting bent out of shape about something, too."

Male, age fifty-four: "No, men can get caught up with stuff women think is 'trivial' . . . like sports scores, scratch or dent the car . . ."

Male, age thirty-five: "Smaller things count more for women than men."

Female, age twenty-nine: "Maybe we don't realize how we're coming across. Basically, we take most stuff in stride, I think."

Male, age seventy-one: "Women are wonderful. They're very emotional and it's wonderful. It brings life to life."

Male, age forty-eight: "Women just *show* certain types of emotions more . . . sentimentality, grief—they don't mask it like we do. Men still feel like they have to look stoic."

Male, age thirty-five: "Women are much more emotional than men. I'd like to think men are starting to become more aware . . . they're learning it from patient women who teach us."

Male, age fifty-three: "Men are more likely to show anger, women to cry."

Female, age twenty-two: "Men don't show emotion, so who knows."

Female, age fifty: "What a silly idea. Men jump out of cars and beat each other up for cutting each other off, and swear vendettas, and gang up against each other in business, and jump up and down and smack each other's backsides when they win a game . . . and they say *we're* emotional?"

The Truth

When it comes to emotions, men and women are equal, though not identical . . . we're *both* emotional. In fact, when it comes to some emotions, men are way ahead of us.

↦ *We both have emotional problems.* Women, as we have mentioned, have a higher risk of depression than men—more than double the risk. Although relationship issues, social learning, and sex roles used to be blamed, most new research is finding it's our hormonal and neurological differences that make women more vulnerable. Dr. Richard Lewine, of Emory University School of Medicine, for example, told the *Atlanta Journal and Constitution* that estrogen may buffer women from schizophrenia (men have twice the rate) but contribute to depression.

And Mark George, M.D., a psychiatrist and neurologist at the NIMH, measured the brain's glucose metabolism to locate activity while men and women had sad thoughts and found, according to *Newsweek*, that women activated eight times more of the part of the brain that processes sadness than men, even though both reported equal amounts of sadness. Researchers speculate that this area becomes overloaded and shuts down eventually, leaving the woman numb and clinically depressed.

More men, however, seem to have a problem with aggression. Men make up the majority of felons, and they kill themselves at more than four times the rate of women.

And the problem often starts early. Emotionally disturbed boys outnumber girls nearly four to one, juvenile male arrests for violent crimes have increased by 50 percent in the last ten years, and the murder rate for male teenagers has gone up more than 100 percent in the past twenty years.

Some scientists speculate the problem males have controlling aggressive feelings relates to the male brain. PET (positron emission tomography) scans show that men have more activity in the temporal-limbic system when their brain is "idling"—that's the part of the brain involved in direct action, often called the "reptilian" or primitive brain. As Sharon Begley, a medical reporter, explains it in *Newsweek*:

"The PET scans may actually be showing that, when told to think of nothing, men fixate on [activities like] sex and football." And what about women? We seem to fixate on words, perhaps even having conversations with ourselves, when our brain is relaxing. We generally show more activity in the more recently evolved part of the brain's limbic system called the *cingulate gyrus*, according to Ruben C. Gur, Ph.D., professor of neuropsychology at the University of Pennsylvania School of Medicine in Philadelphia. That may mean we're more likely to postpone aggression and think before we act.

↔ *We both get angry.* Although men may have a greater problem managing and controlling aggression, women get angry just as often. Perhaps the largest study of anger, by psychologist Charles D. Spielberger, Ph.D., of the University of South Florida, polled 3,600 adults and found males and females equally likely to experience anger on a daily basis. But women, he states, are more likely to try to understand the cause of others' behaviors while men are more likely to act on their anger.

Psychologist Sandra Thomas studied more than 500 women for her book, *Women and Anger*, and also found that, as a rule, few women (9 percent) directly confront the object of their anger. But 75 percent say they wouldn't hold back anger with a family member, and 91 percent would express it to a friend.

↔ *We both read minds.* Dr. Gur and neuroscientist Raquel Gur, M.D., Ph.D., his wife, also used the PET scan to research differences in how well women and men read emotions on people's faces. They found that both sexes read happy expressions perfectly well. They also found that both sexes also recognized sadness on men's faces 90 percent of the time. When it came to reading sad expressions on women's faces, however, men were wrong about 30 percent of the time, even though the PET scan showed their brains were working harder at the task than women's brains!

This may explain the major difference between men and women when it comes to reading and reacting to others. Our clinical findings at the Stress Program at Mount Sinai School of Medicine in New York is that women usually do it with empathy, and men with sympathy. Sympathy is the ability to care about the feelings. In practice, this means most men ask to be told what a woman is feeling and what he can do to help. But empathy is the ability to experience the feelings of another person, so women often *know* what's wrong and exactly what would help. When women assume men could do this too "if they really loved us" or "if they really tried," they're often mistaken! Studies say communication improves when couples state their needs clearly and give up the notion that "it doesn't count if I have to ask."

↦ *We both have anxiety.* Although both sexes suffer from anxiety, women are more likely to recognize the emotion, label it, and seek professional or medical help, according to research we reported in the updated *Male Stress Syndrome*. Men, on the other hand, were more likely to label anxiety symptoms such as headaches, stomachaches, or heavy breathing as fatigue or flu symptoms and say they'd rather go to a dentist than see a psychotherapist.

↦ *We both cry* . . . until we're about twelve years old, that is. Then girls begin to cry more frequently, and after age eighteen, according to the Ramsey Clinic Dry Eye and Tear Research Center in St. Paul, we cry four times as frequently as men. But don't jump to the conclusion that it's all society's fault. Emotional tears (compared to tears after an eye irritation) contain the hormone called *prolactin*. This is the hormone that promotes milk for breast-feeding, and by age eighteen, females have 60 percent more of this hormone in their bloodstream than males. So our crying level may reflect more nature than nurture. Or it may reflect our willingness to admit to crying. After all, the center found that 71 percent of men did report "watery eyes" and 73 percent of men said they felt better after crying.

↦ *Women are not less rational.* We may *show* more emotion when we're upset, but a study conducted by Marianne LaFrance of Boston College and Mahzarin Banaji of Yale University found men probably *feel* more upset. Their heart rate, blood pressure, rate of respiration, and nervous system all go through greater changes than ours when they're under stress. And psychologist Janet Shibley Hyde, Ph.D., points out in *Half the Human Experience* that females usually *excel* on verbal reasoning tests, and there is no research support for the idea that women are less logical or less rational than men.

↦ *Women are not crazed victims of PMS.* PMS doesn't turn

women into emotional hurricanes. In one study conducted by the EDK Forecast Group, 59 percent of women said they notice the upset of PMS but can live with it, and 10 percent said they feel little or no effect. That means only 31 percent say it affects their life at all, and no more than 3 to 5 percent of all PMS sufferers have debilitating symptoms. As for that famous statistic that about 45 percent of criminal acts committed by women occur during the premenstrual or menstrual period, Janet Shibley Hyde explains that the premenstrual and menstrual period covers eight or nine days, and we could expect at least 38 percent of female crimes to be committed during *any* eight- or nine-day period. And the male crime rate during any nine-day period is still higher than the female crime rate during the premenstrual period.

Besides, the irritability some women feel premenstrually is assumed to be associated with a drop in the pacifying hormones estrogen and progesterone, leaving the effects of our testosterone unbuffered. That probably means we behave for a few days a month *more like men behave all month long!*

Not that testosterone automatically makes one aggressive, but studies have found that among college wrestlers there are higher testosterone levels in winners than in losers! Aggressive hockey players had more testosterone than their more easygoing teammates. And aggressive prisoners had almost double the testosterone of the average male not in prison. In other studies, however, testosterone did not correlate at all with aggressive behavior. It is unlikely that hormones alone dictate our emotional profiles; they may, instead, set our *thresholds* for reactions—perhaps our readiness for certain emotional responses.

↦ *Women are not crazed victims of menopause.* Just fifteen years ago, the diagnostic manual of the American Psychiatric Association still included "involutional melancholia," a depression assumed to be triggered by menopause. And for some, that turned into a self-fulfilling prophecy, of course. But for most women, menopause is a minor inconvenience at worst, as we pointed out in Chapter 2.

Here are some statistics from *Consumer Reports on Health*, 1994:

—About 75 percent of menopausal women experience hot flashes (sudden rushes of heat that leave them sweating), but only 10 to 15 percent find them disruptive, more than two thirds of women don't even mention them to their physician, and four out of five women say they disappear within two years.

—An ongoing University of Pennsylvania study finds *no* evidence of increased anger, instability, nervousness, self-consciousness, or excitability before or during menopause. In fact, the only symptoms most studies find are fatigue and irritability after those nights when hot flashes and sweating interfered with a good night's sleep.

—A Massachusetts study of more than 2,000 menopausal women and a six-year Swedish study of 900 middle-aged women both found *no* increased risk of depression or any other mental disorder before or during menopause. Women who did get depressed during this period had lost a parent, gone through a divorce, lost a job, or developed an illness.

—At least two sex surveys done in 1995, by *Parade* magazine and the University of Chicago, find middle-aged women have *no* loss of sexual capacity. The Consumers Union research reports 95 percent of married women in their fifties are still sexually active, 88 percent of unmarried women are also, and in another study, 94 percent of sexually inactive women said they would be interested if they could find a partner! (See Chapter 2 for related figures.)

How to Use the Truth

We are all capable of emotion, and from a strictly scientific point of view, emotions have survival value: Anxiety warns us of danger, fear teaches us how to avoid it, infatuation helps us overcome commitment concerns, and love bonds us so we can help each other survive and thrive.

But although women are not more emotional than men, we are individuals with individual differences in emotions as in other things. And like men, we, too, can need help managing some emotions.

•• *Start with a medical checkup.* Anyone—man, woman, or child—who begins to lose a sense of control and choice about emotional behavior needs a medical checkup first. Anger, irritability, anxiety, mood swings, depression ... this long list of psychological symptoms can often be the result of physical problems, particularly if there is no identifiable precipitating event.

Feelings of despair or depression, for example, may really be the result of:

 —anemia
 —virus aftermath (the washed-out feeling can last longer than we expect)
 —medication side effects
 —drug abuse symptoms
 —nutritional deficiencies
 —central nervous system disorders (including multiple sclerosis, strokes)
 —and hormonal disorders, to name a few.

Anxiety sensations may really be physical signs of:

 —mitral valve prolapse
 —low blood pressure
 —low blood sugar
 —medication reactions
 —overuse of stimulants (including coffee, nicotine, and some colas)
 —drug dependency or withdrawal symptoms
 —and other medical problems

Irritability and anger may be signs of:

 —thyroid problems
 —sleep deprivation or apnea
 —chronic pain
 —caffeine or nicotine abuse or withdrawal
 —medication dosage problems

These are some examples.

In other words, if emotions have suddenly gone wild, a thorough checkup may find a reason . . . not an excuse, a reason. If you check out medically, it's time to help yourself.

 ↦ *Manage PMS.* Women are told either that raging hormones make us irrational or that the symptoms are all in our head. They can't both be true. In fact, neither's true! The latest research finds what *is* in our heads is probably a premenstrual decrease in mood-elevating brain chemicals like *serotonin,* and that alone can create many of the symptoms of PMS, which include:

—carbohydrate cravings

—mood swings or depression

—anxiety

—anger and irritability

—sleep disturbances

—headaches

—bloating and breast tenderness

—fatigue

Even though researchers haven't pinpointed all the causes, they've found ways to help control PMS:

—First, get a medical checkup to rule out diabetes, anemia, thyroid problems, and ovarian growths, which can cause similar problems.

—Then keep a diary of your symptoms for at least two months to be sure they're cycle-related. If the symptoms occur randomly or last for more than two weeks a month, the problem isn't PMS! But if it is PMS, then try the following suggestions from reproductive endocrinologists:

  • *If you gain weight, cut back on salt and alcohol.*
    They increase water retention.

  • *If you become anxious, nervous, sleepless, or have*
    breast tenderness, wean yourself off caffeine . . .
    it makes all these symptoms worse.

—For food cravings, some experts say to eat a small amount of complex carbohydrates like pasta or grains every three hours to boost serotonin, a brain chemical that can ease stress, or you'll grab for chocolate. High-carbo meals may soothe depression, tension, anger, confusion, and sadness, and increase alertness and calmness. (This may explain why women with PMS crave carbohydrates.)

—And to steady your mood and counteract insomnia and depression, a new report in the *Journal of Psychosomatic Research* says to exercise at least four times a week, especially through the winter. It raises levels of endorphin, our natural mood elevator, in the brain.

—There's evidence that de-stressing via yoga, meditation, and relaxation techniques reduces both mind and body symptoms.

—Some women take vitamin B$_6$ for two weeks before their menses, but physicians warn that you must not take more than 100 milligrams or nerve damage could result. B$_{12}$ and magnesium appear to be less potentially dangerous, but according to studies are less effective. Remember to see your doctor before undertaking vitamin therapy.

For women with more severe symptoms such as immobilizing depression and tremendous emotional upheavals, a psychiatrist specializing in psychopharmacology may prescribe antidepressants or antianxiety drugs. These drugs can raise spirits enough to permit daily functioning and raise the motivation capacity for psychotherapy, too!

Now, about 2 to 5 percent of all PMS sufferers have such debilitating symptoms that these tips alone won't do it. If that's you, show your diary to your physician or contact a PMS clinic. They can offer support groups, behavior modification, hormone therapy for headaches, or one of many new prescription drugs for very severe mood swings.

↪ *Manage "sensitivity" and hurt feelings.* Psychologists classify as many as 10 to 15 percent of us as very sensitive. That means particularly empathetic and perceptive about people's behaviors and emotions, more compliant than competitive, *almost* "too good," prone to cry easily, and likely to take everything very personally, from gestures to comments. But don't blame yourself. You were probably born with tendencies toward that temperament. You can, however, increase or decrease your sensitivity, so here are tips:

—First, try not to overprotect yourself or see yourself as weak. Others will pick up on it.

—If you cry in public, do it in a matter-of-fact way. And later, when you're home, figure out what you can say or do instead of crying, and rehearse it!

—Finally, to ease the hurt when you're taking things personally, refocus, instead, on what you can learn about others from their behavior . . . who's nice, who's jealous, who's a bully. This isn't easy, because sensitive people find rudeness and criticism particularly difficult, but it's worth practicing. I used to tell my daughter: "Everything other people say and do is information about them, not you."

We reviewed criticism in the chapter about self-esteem (Chapter 1), so let's move on to rudeness. If it's rudeness, label it. Say "That sounds like an insult" or "That's a hurtful thing to say." You're not attacking the other person, just the statement, so you'll usually get a correction or explanation. If you don't, ask for one. Ask for clarification: "What do you mean by that?" or "Excuse me, I don't understand." It addresses the rudeness without being defensive and puts rude people on the spot to explain. Actually, they may have a point to make, but you'll be letting them know that it needs rephrasing.

If they persist, you can ask about their intentions: "Are you trying to make me feel bad?" You can ask about their motivation: "Why are you being rude to me?" And if there are others around, you can get group pressure going by asking for a second opinion, like: "Anyone else think this is out of line?"

The point is that being sensitive when someone else is rude doesn't mean being weak. So if words fail, use a silent stare to say you're not participating, allow yourself to get teary if that's how you feel—and if it's appropriate—and let the other person feel bad or, as a last resort, leave.

↔ *Manage fear.* The capacity for fear is important. Fear can provide the adrenaline to cope with a new situation or emergency. It heightens the senses, makes thinking faster and more precise, and gives us a boost of energy . . . to a point. When the adrenaline gets too high, however, fear can be paralyzing and numbing. So let's talk about bringing fear down to a manageable level or reducing it completely.

The trick is often to think of your fear as potentially working to your advantage and *not* as a signal to run the other way. If fear is standing between you and something you want to do or have to do, acknowledge your fear and *do it anyway.* Your fear will become diluted, you'll become desensitized, and your learning curve will be high!

Since two national surveys list fear of public speaking above the fear of death, let's use this fear as an example. For women, public speaking is not just a concern of female CEOs. It's wedding toasts and PTA reports that undo us. But you really can help yourself. Let's start with some techniques from experts who train public speakers:

—First, they all say to rehearse! Practice out loud, alone, even if you feel silly. That way, the speech itself becomes easy and familiar, and you become relaxed with the sound of your own voice.

—Then, many suggest a technique called *desensitization.* You start by getting comfortable, breathe slowly and easily, and let all the muscles in your neck and shoulders relax.

—Next, while you're relaxed, imagine the first tiny step toward giving a speech, like the image of getting dressed that morning. When you can stay relaxed with that image, go on to the next . . . like walking toward the stage, then standing in front of the audience, and so forth. If you feel even the slightest fear at any step, go back to an image you've already desensitized, relax, and try again. About fifteen minutes a day for a week or two usually makes an enormous difference.

When you're actually in front of the audience: Focus on the audience and what you want to tell them instead of focusing on yourself and how you sound. Make lots of eye contact. Studies find that speakers who avoid eye contact are seen as insecure, dishonest, or not interested in their own subject. Never apologize for nervousness, mistakes, or noise . . . it makes the audience worry for you instead of listening to you. And always act confident even if you don't feel that way. The audience will take cues from you.

If you still feel nervous about public speaking, give yourself permission to be less than perfect and do it anyway! If everyone let nervousness stop them, nobody would be a public speaker, because *everyone* gets nervous at first. Television anchor and trainer Julie Ekhart recommends talking to a few women beforehand to establish rapport, and then looking for their "friendly faces" while speaking.

↪ *Manage anger.* To fight or not to fight when you're angry—it's confusing. Popular advice for a decade has been to share our feelings with the "significant others" in our lives. If they care about you, givers of this advice conclude, they will understand and take your emotion as a sign of deep caring. But if you've practiced yelling and tried out the "new honesty" approach, you've probably found that there were few people around who respected your anger or took it as a sign of deep caring. More likely, as we mentioned in Chapter 3, you found that your angry outbursts led others to defensiveness, withdrawal, or angry outbursts of their own, and led you to more anger. That's because fighting has a *practice effect.* Yelling today is practice for a second shouting match tomorrow, and a second fight increases the risk of a third, and so on. Each time you let it all hang out, you lower your threshold for doing it again. And remember, you also act as a model for those around you, and have lowered *their* threshold for yelling, too. Furthermore, you probably provide them with an excuse for focusing their day's frustrations with commuting, working, and conforming, on you!

Then, too, adrenaline released during battle triggers the "fight or flight" response, not a logical thought response. The fight response can lead to physical abuse, and the flight response to job walkouts and separations, all difficult or impossible situations to mend. In the short run, then, fighting may feel good—but in the long run, fighting only leads to more fighting.

Am I suggesting that you swallow your anger or bottle up your furies instead? That wasn't my recommendation for Type A women and it's not my recommendation now. But what I do suggest is that the expression of all-out rage is a self-indulgence, a luxury that should be reserved for your private moments alone. If you want to grab a pillow by two corners and beat the bed with it, do it! If you feel like writing a scathing letter and then ripping it into little pieces, do it! If you need to run, walk, pedal, swim, or chop wood until you've used up the adrenaline that poured out when your fight-or-flight button was pushed, do it!

Then, after you've privately vented your impulse to destroy, search your psyche until you can honestly explain your anger to yourself. Most of us find that our anger usually means we've been insulted by someone who matters to us; we've been criticized about something we often criticize ourselves about; we've been ignored by someone we care about; or we've been frustrated by unexpected demands.

Next, try to review the situation to see what you can learn about yourself from the conflict—and about your adversary as well. Use that information to formulate the communication you want to express. Here are some suggestions on how to start:

—Tailor your communication for the particular person you're angry with. Speak to them in language they can understand. Don't assume your husband, your boss, your secretary, or your best friend will hear you the same way, or that they're sensitive in exactly the same way that you're sensitive. If you find that you're always sounding off with the same complaints and phrases, your communication is clearly not effective.

—Sentences beginning with "I" were discussed in the self-esteem chapter. They sound less accusing than statements starting with the word "you." "You" sentences usually attack other people or suggest you can read their mind. They then become defensive, withdrawn, or too angry themselves to care about your feelings. For example, "I feel so sad when you flirt with other women" is more likely to inspire your partner to give you reassurance than a statement like "You make a fool of yourself and me by flirting all the time." The "you" statement is more likely to begin a rebuttal and counteraccusation instead—in other words, a fight!

—Decide before you get involved in a discussion that can lead to a fight exactly what you want or need from the other person. Then find the words to ask for it. Your aim, presumably, is to make yourself feel better after the discussion. If a hug, an answer, or more time is what you need, for example, don't wait for the process of mental telepathy to be perfected. To test love by expecting a mate to read your mind is to invite a disappointment—and another fight.

—If all this fails and you find yourself yelling anyway, promise yourself that you'll try not to stray from the issue at hand or say things that both of you would prefer to be forgotten afterward. And if you think things said in anger can later be forgotten, think again. You probably remember hurts forever, and so does everyone else.

The final word on fights? If your aim is to make things better, not worse, don't use your fighting skills on your friends or lovers. Use your abilities to negotiate, clarify, request, and assess instead. That way you'll all come out ahead.

↔ *Count to ten with children.* Perhaps the most frequent requests I get from television viewers are mothers' letters asking for tips on how to keep their temper under control. This doesn't mean mothers should never become angry at children's behavior, set limits, or teach logical consequences. It means that when we are irritable, tired, worried, or in pain we may overreact. So if children are complaining about each other ("Roy won't let me watch my program") and you're busy, just repeat their complaints to let them know you've heard ("Roy won't let you watch your program") but don't plan to get involved. They'll usually get tired and give up quickly. It works! Or surprise them by laughing when they expect yelling, or giving them a big kiss in front of their friends. They'll usually leave you alone for a while.

—Now if the noise level gets to you, physiologists say, a relaxation technique like meditation, yoga, or biofeedback can change your tolerance threshold in twenty seconds.

—But if it's the constant contact, take a break if someone can watch the children. Just twenty minutes of reading, exercise, or a warm bath can feel like a two-hour nap.

—Or, if you can't take a break, telephone a friend to hear an adult voice. But ask for a joke instead of complaining, or you'll still be angry when you hang up.

—Most important, if you start in a bad mood, warn your children. It teaches them about emotions, and unless you're in a bad mood all the time, they're usually smart about it.

If you're really afraid of losing control, the National Committee to Prevent Child Abuse suggests you distract yourself immediately so your rage doesn't keep building to a breaking point. Go to a door or window and take a deep breath, splash water on your face, drink a glass of water, press your lips together and count to ten (or twenty) . . . close your eyes and imagine how you're going to sound to a child, or just walk out of the room (not the house—that would feel like abandonment to the child). Always remind yourself that you are the adult, and your children will learn to handle their temper exactly as you do.

If you really do lose control, find professional help immediately through your family physician or the National Committee to Prevent Child Abuse. Physical or psychological violence is never a do-it-yourself treatment project.

↪ ***Manage anxiety attacks.*** Two thirds of all people who suffer from anxiety attacks or panic disorders are women, according to the Anxiety Disorders Association of America. The symptoms seem to appear out of the blue (usually when we're in our twenties, although new research from Stanford Medical Center reports unidentified attacks often begin as early as the fifth or seventh grade), and are not imaginary, self-induced, or caused by everyday stress.

Typically, the episode begins with heart palpitations, shortness of breath, and a sense of choking. Researchers suspect that these symptoms are usually preceded by hyperventilation (rapid breathing) that was unnoticed, and the resulting drop in blood levels of carbon dioxide triggers the increase in heart rate. This change in blood chemistry also seems to stimulate the primitive "fear" center of the brain, and a sense of impending doom combines with the physical symptoms. Is it any wonder that people think they're having a heart attack, going crazy, or going to die? Those feelings, of course, increase the hyperventilation and add adrenaline into the mix. The symptoms "cascade" into a cycle.

The attack usually lasts for several minutes but can go on much longer. The signs may include any of these:

—shortness of breath or a smothering sensation

—dizziness, lightheadedness, unsteady feelings, or faintness

—palpitations or accelerated heart rate

—trembling or shaking

—sweating

—choking

—nausea or abdominal distress

—dreamlike sensations or perceptual distortions, including a sense of depersonalization or of unreality

—numbness or tingling, especially in the hands

—hot flashes or chills

—chest pain or discomfort

—terror—a sense that something unimaginably horrible is about to occur and that one is powerless to prevent it

—fear of going crazy or of losing control and doing something embarrassing

—fear of dying

Sometimes, fear of having a panic attack brings on an attack! It's important to realize that *everyone* feels the symptoms listed above occasionally and that they do go away. If you experience the symptoms frequently, a medical checkup can reassure you that the symptoms are not part of a heart attack and can break the cycle so panic can't keep feeding on itself. A checkup is particularly necessary since women with mitral valve prolapse (congenital "floppy" heart valve—a condition much more common in women than in men) seem to be at a higher risk for developing this syndrome during hyperventilation than the general population, though not all people with MVP do. It's important that all sufferers remember that these attacks are based on biochemical changes and physical characteristics, and not label themselves fearful or neurotic.

Take this quiz if you think you may have anxiety attacks. Answer "true" or "false" to each statement.

ANXIETY-LEVEL INVENTORY

1. ___ Sometimes my heart rate is high, although my medical checkup was fine.
2. ___ I often have a hard time falling asleep.
3. ___ Sometimes I hyperventilate until I feel like I can't breathe.
4. ___ Sometimes my lips or fingers feel numb or tingle for no reason.
5. ___ I often fear that I might faint, although I never do.

Even one symptom suggests you're dealing with some anxiety. If you answered "true" to two or more, the quality of your life is probably being compromised, and it's time to start managing the problem.

There are many ways of handling panic disorder, and it's important to do so, before fear of the attacks creates phobias that begin to limit life choices and lifestyle.

—Some therapists help the patient *create* the attack in the office (by hyperventilating or pumping up heart rate) and then explain every symptom while it happens in order to remove the terror of the unknown. The patient, of course, also gets to see that she has survived the attack, that the therapist was calm and unworried, and that the attack stopped sooner when it was treated matter-of-factly.

—Many patients are taught breathing techniques that can prevent or quickly reverse hyperventilation and its effects. In fact, the breathing technique on page 41 is effective for this. Review it and try it. If you can't get the hang of it yourself, try biofeedback training. A computer monitor gives you continual feedback, so you can practice until you know you're doing it correctly.

—Regular exercise can prevent many attacks (particularly for

MVP patients) by burning up the extra adrenaline that can trigger the hyperventilation or palpitations, or by conditioning you so you're less apt to hyperventilate.

You can take your choice of exercises that can help prevent some panic attacks:

—Walking. It's the most common choice for women of all ages.

—Calisthenics. About one in five women twenty to forty-four years old work out at home or in health clubs.

—Swimming. Fifteen percent of women surveyed report swimming.

—Jogging. It's popular but, as with all strenuous exercise, check with your physician first.

Other cathartic activities are competitive: tennis, racquetball, paddleball, team sports, marathons, games like backgammon and cards. They all can potentially work! The trick is to try them and then *do* them.

—Medications like beta-blockers diminish the severity of the cardiovascular symptoms of the disorder, anxiety-relieving drugs control the hyperventilation and fearful sensations, and some anti-depressant medication changes the brain biochemistry. These are prescription medications that can be prescribed by a psychiatrist. The disorder is not a type of heart problem, neurosis, or depression, however. Each of these medications has effects useful for treating panic disorder, despite their labels associated with other diagnoses.

↝ *Manage anticipatory anxiety.* Many men and women are experts in dread. We worry about our jobs, our children, our health, our attractiveness, and a long list of other important life aspects long before any problems arise. It's true that some anticipatory emotions can help prevent problems—people who worry, researchers have noted, actually have a survival advantage! But it isn't appropriate to live in constant anxiety or fear. To help manage bothersome anticipatory emotions:

—Separate fact from fiction: What's worth worrying about? What isn't? Many of us can cut our "To Worry About" list in half with this simple step.

—Log the unpleasant time spent in anticipatory emotions. The numbers of minutes, even hours, may shock you! Then resolve to pass this wasted time in some more productive way—and start doing it.

—If anticipatory emotions are unavoidable, put the adrenaline they produce into action. Are we worried that our child will take daredevil risks on her bicycle? Put on a coat, go out into the street with her, teach her the rules of the road, show her a squashed soda can or acorn in the road to make the dangers perfectly clear, give her some tips, and then cheer her on.

↦ *Manage the blahs.* Even though women are *not* "too emotional," we do get tired, discouraged, temporarily down. If you're feeling down:

—Look for people who are up. Forget about "misery loves company" because bad moods are catching.

—Spare the people who are your support system. Don't attack them or you'll drive them away.

—Decide what you need to feel better, and ask for it: a movie, flowers, a backrub . . .

—Don't allow yourself to say, "Anything is better than this." My patients often use that as an excuse for chocolate binges, shopping binges, alcohol, and affairs. You'll soon have more problems than feeling down! Exercise is usually the best quick fix.

↦ *Manage depression.* We so often use the term "depressed" when we're "down" that we don't always recognize and treat a real depression. This test, based on warning signs identified by researchers at Harvard, the American Psychiatric Association, and the National Depressive and Manic-Depressive Association, will help you see if you may have some signs of depression. Place a check mark next to any statement that applies to you.

DEPRESSIVE-SIGNS QUIZ

1. ___ I feel down almost all the time.
2. ___ Things that used to bring me pleasure don't anymore.
3. ___ I often think the world would be a better place if I were dead.
4. ___ Nobody wants me, nobody needs me, I'm no help at all.
5. ___ I'm losing weight without being on a diet.
6. ___ I wake up during the night for no reason.

7. __ I feel restless and jumpy.
8. __ I can't think as clearly as I used to.
9. __ I'm tired even when I've had a decent night's sleep.
10. __ I feel no hope about the future.

As you may have guessed, all of the above can be signs of depression. If you checked off at least five of the statements, including the first or second one, and if you've been feeling that way for at least two weeks, make an appointment with a licensed mental health professional. If you checked off the third statement, get help right away! Depression is biochemical—a *medical* condition that can be treated. At least four out of five depressed people feel much better after brief psychotherapy and/or antidepressant medication. In fact, a National Institute of Mental Health study found that whereas drug therapy brought quicker, more effective relief to people who were depressed, short-term "talk" therapy worked almost as well, without side-effects.

You should know that some people swing from depression to a high-energy phase called mania—the condition is called *manic depression* (or *bipolar illness*). Warning signs of mania may include:

—ultra-high energy levels
—much less need for sleep
—overconfidence in abilities
—inappropriate elation
—increased talkativeness, agitation, and excessive sexual activity
—racing thoughts
—impulsive behavior

See a mental health professional for all forms of depression.

You should know, too, that depression can cause physical symptoms such as headaches or backaches; a doctor who's not a mental health specialist may never suspect that depression is at the root of them. A 1989 study by the Rand Corporation found that doctors miss the diagnosis of severe depression at least half the time.

↦ *Manage sadness.* Sadness and depression are not the same. Depression is triggered by internal emotional or biological forces within us, but sadness is usually triggered by a real-life event—loss of someone we love, loss of health, loss of a job or job opportunity. Depression usually doesn't vary much over twenty-four hours, but sadness tends to grow worse at the end of the day. Depression wakes us up early and interferes with sleep, but sadness makes us want to escape into sleep.

If someone you care about is going through a period of sadness:

—Don't take over for her. Too much advice or help can lower her self-confidence and overwhelm her. Help her to help herself instead.

—Don't push her into activities too soon. Just let her know they're there when she's ready.

—Do watch for depression. It's normal to feel sorry for yourself for a while after a loss. If she loses her appetite, awakens early, and develops many physical complaints, encourage her to consult her doctor or to seek professional counseling.

—Do keep her company. Even silent company offers her a needed sense of security and caring.

If it's you who are sad, allow the people who care about you to help you. Your sadness may not disappear, but loneliness won't be added. And it may help to remember that some mourning is normal if the loss is serious and that it takes time to accept the fact that we were not able to control events.

So find opportunities to talk about your grief out loud. As you hear your own words, you may get some distance from your pain and put your loss into a wider perspective. And beyond talk, sadness passes. Faith helps some. Love helps us all.

↤ ***Don't underestimate faith.*** Faith is so universal that most social scientists assume it meets a basic human need. Faith can help you feel confident that you can handle whatever life brings and help you accept situations you can't control. And if your faith includes prayer, those quiet pauses can slow down your body's flight-or-fight response . . . and that can lower your blood pressure and heart rate, reduce insomnia, and even change your pain threshold.

And if you don't have a religious faith but you want many of its benefits, you don't have to look to the mystical.

—Meditate. It brings many of the benefits of prayer. Find a quiet spot, a comfortable position, deeply relax your muscles and then focus on the rhythm of your breathing for ten minutes. Tests at Harvard's Thorndike Memorial Lab say this kind of meditation can give you more energy and less insomnia, and can often relieve some of the stress that leads to high blood pressure.

—Donate. If you are missing the sense of community that an organized religion can give you, try donating time to a charity, maybe help someone you haven't even met yet. You'll probably feel part of something larger than yourself.

—Contemplate. If you've squeezed wonder and curiosity out of your life, put them back in. Look at the immense night sky or listen to great music or let the shower water run over you until your perspective shifts and your problems seem small . . . and hold on to it.

↪ *Create positive emotions.* Even though creating good feelings helps us counteract the bad, many of us are as uncomfortable with our positive emotions as our negative ones. There are many reasons:

Some of us avoid good feelings because we suspect that if we feel happy today, we'll pay the price in sadness tomorrow. In truth, we know no one is keeping tabs on our good feelings—we can indulge in them as often as we like! We can't have them every moment for the rest of our lives, because our bodies and minds would become exhausted. But we are entitled to as many good feelings as we can create.

Some of us avoid good feelings because all strong emotions—positive ones included—can make us fear being swept away with their power, out of control, or unprepared for a new experience. It may help to think of new emotions as opportunities for new points of view. It may help to remember that strong emotions can't last forever, anyway. Actually, some of us avoid good feelings for that very reason—because we don't want to feel disappointed when they go. Knowing we can recreate them again and again may help. So start recognizing opportunities for experiences that give you good feelings. You can master a new skill, find someone new to love, have an adventure. . . . You get the idea.

COUNTERING THE MYTH OF
THE OVERWROUGHT WOMAN

We are all emotional. So let emotions give your life texture.

If you're told *women* are too emotional, **discuss it**. Ask for the data, then provide the real information.

If you're told *you're* too emotional, **consider it**. Ask yourself what it says about them as well as about you.

If you're told *girls* are too emotional, **counter it**. Help the girls you love learn to deal with the emotions that frighten or bother them. Help them learn to create more of the emotions they enjoy. And help them learn what they need to know to fight the stereotype of the "too emotional" female.

CHAPTER 7

The Myth:

*"Women
are not
mechanical"*

The Myth:

- Women rarely fix anything around the house.
- We're intuitive, not logical.
- Women have very little concept of how a car—or any machine—works.
- We need a man around to explain computers and VCR settings.
- Females in general are bad at math and science.
- We're rarely inventors.
- We aren't interested in building things.
- We aren't good at navigating our way from one place to another and can't even read a map.
- Diagrams make us dizzy.

Who Believes It?

It's probably no shock that most men say the stereotype is true, "Women aren't very mechanical," while women say, "Yes, we are."

Let's first see what the opposite sex says:

Sixty-seven percent of all men responding to our PRODIGY Poll answered in the affirmative, "Women aren't very mechanical." Only 27 percent said it's not true, and just 6 percent said they're not sure. Among single men, 59 percent buy into the myth and 68 percent of all married men believe it to be true. And divorced, separated, and widowed men are the strongest believers in the stereotype (71 percent).

The majority of the women, on the other hand, rejected the stereotype (64 percent). Sixty-two percent of the divorced women, 63 percent of the single women, and 70 percent of the married women say the stereotype is wrong. Actually, widowed women were the only marital group in which the majority did buy the myth (52 percent).

It seems to be a generational trend when we look at age-related responses. Perhaps young women are more handy, or less afraid to demonstrate their skill. Or older men could do more mechanically or insisted on doing more mechanically. Whatever the reasons, the older we are, the more we believe that women aren't as mechanical as men. In the under-twenty-five age group, just 44 percent of men and women buy into the myth. From age twenty-five to age forty-four, that number increases to 52 percent. It rises to 63 percent among the forty-five-plus crowd.

Men from all occupations believe women to be less mechanical, and women in most occupations don't. But it may surprise you to find out that 44 percent of the women in our sample who actually work as mechanics or in closely related fields *do* believe the myth.

The non-computer-based local surveys and interviews confirm that most men believe they're more mechanical than women, and most women say they're just as mechanical as men (or they're not sure about this one).

The quotes spell it out more clearly:

Female, age thirty-one: "I *tell* my husband he's handy so he'll do more around the house!"

Female, age fifty-two: "If I waited for a man to fix everything, I'd be living in the dark and in the cold."

Male, forty: "I think men are just more interested in building buildings and bridges and cars. Women could do it, but they don't."

Female, age forty-eight: "Depends what you mean by 'mechanical.' I can read a manual. Maybe men don't have to."

Female, age twenty-two: "My mother is so helpless . . . it's always 'the man from the repair shop' or 'the man from the telephone company' or 'the man from the garage' who she calls."

My best friend, Connie: "I have my own power tools . . . what does that tell you?"

The Truth

Are women mechanically disadvantaged? Are we mathematical dunces? Computer-challenged? Scientific research is providing some surprising answers:

↔ **Boys and girls have equal problem-solving ability.** Data from California high schools between 1983 and 1987 indicate that girls and boys taking advanced science courses were equally adept at problem solving. What about the differences between the male and female brain? The one we hear about most often is that experts say women tend to have a thicker corpus callosum, a band of nerve fibers that connects the brain's right and left side. Women may be using both hemispheres to problem-solve and men may be favoring their left or right side. The implications, however, are not clear. It may simply mean that women and men go about their thinking in different ways, women more "globally," men in a more linear way. Research continues . . .

↔ **Girls and boys have equal math ability.** The difference between male and female math aptitude is so close to zero that we should consider it zero, says Janet Shibley Hyde in her book *Half the Human Experience*.

↔ **Girls do better in math class.** Girls get higher grades than boys in math class in spite of the fact that, as the AAUW study mentioned in Chapter One says, they have traditionally gotten less attention and encouragement from math teachers.

↔ **Women can navigate.** Women and men find their way in different ways. Thomas G. Bever, Ph.D., and colleagues at the University of Rochester have led blindfolded women and men through a maze of tunnels beneath the university. When Bever asked the still-blindfolded subjects where they were at various stopping points, women were better at describing local landmarks—stairs, Coke machine, a large pipe with a valve—while men were better at showing their general location by pointing to the campus library.

↦ ***Girls like science.*** Data from California high schools in the 1980s showed girls make up 38 percent of physics students, 34 percent of advanced physics students, and 42 percent of chemistry students.

↦ ***Women are inventive.*** Most of us don't know that women hold 80,000 or more patents in the United States. Women invented Liquid Paper, the Melitta coffee filter system, the Kevlar material used for bulletproof vests, and much more. A review of the "mothers of invention," by Sue Smith-Heavenrich for *Mothering* (June 22, 1994), and several other sources tell us:

—Marie Curie discovered a way to extract radioactive material from ore in 1898.

—Catherine Littlefield Greene came up with the original idea for the cotton gin. Her houseguest, Eli Whitney, apparently put her idea into practice—and got the credit.

—Olive Dennis designed a ventilation system for trains in the 1920s that fed clean fresh air to individual passengers without disturbing neighbors.

—Marjorie Joyner, a black beautician, invented a permanent-wave machine in 1928.

—Katherine Blodgett was the first woman scientist hired by General Electric. She developed non-reflecting glass in 1938.

—Helen Brooke Taussig developed a heart-bypass method in the 1940s for "blue babies" who were not getting enough oxygen.

—Chien-shiung Wu discovered that electrons emitted from a radioactive nucleus had direction, and she worked on the Manhattan Project. Later she helped in the understanding of sickle-cell anemia.

—Rachel Brown and Elizabeth Lee Hazen discovered a substance in a cow pasture that eventually became the antifungal medicine Nystatin in 1948.

—Betty Nesmith Graham was an error-prone typist who learned

basic chemistry and tested white compounds in her garage until she came up with one that covered mistakes, dried quickly, and accepted the ink of an overtype. Liquid Paper was born in the late 1950s.

—Grace Hopper, Ph.D., created a computer element that changes English into a form a computer can understand. She also was a developer of COBOL, a computer language.

—Gladys A. Emerson isolated vitamin E in wheat germ oil.

—Rosalyn Yalow, Ph.D., developed the radioimmunoassay, a technique for measuring tiny concentrations of biological substances or drugs in the blood or other body fluid in the 1950s. In 1977 she became the first American woman to win the Nobel Prize for medicine.

—Ruth Wakefield is credited with the creation of the chocolate chip cookie.

—Ann Moore designed the Snugli baby carrier in the 1960s, after she was in the Peace Corps in Africa and had seen how contented African babies were when carried on their mothers' backs.

—Dr. Maria Goeppert-Mayer was part of a team that helped perfect the atom bomb.

—Gertrude Elion developed drugs for treating cancer and viruses. She won the 1988 Nobel Prize in medicine.

—And Hedy Lamarr (star of the 1933 movie *Ecstasy*) invented an antijamming device, used against Nazi radar in the 1940s and used by satellite communication systems today.

Says Chips Klein, co-director (and a woman) of the Women Inventors Project, a Toronto educational and consulting group that corrects misconceptions about inventions: "We know that women inventors were there in history. We know what they came up with, but support for them just wasn't there."

Fewer than 2 percent of the more than four million patents on file in the U.S. are under a woman's name because their fathers, husbands, or male colleagues have typically received the recognition. The 1990 edition of the *Encyclopedia Americana* cites more than 150 inventors; *not one* is a woman. The same is true of the 1992 edition of the *World Book Encyclopedia,* reports Smith-Heavenrich. The Women Inventors Project is just one of many programs that hope to change all that. Sue

Smith-Heavenrich quotes Nobel laureate Rosalyn Yalow: "The world cannot afford the loss of the talents of half its people if we are to solve the many problems which beset us."

↦ **Women are closing the math gap.** The SATs (Scholastic Aptitude Tests) can tell us a lot about how society is changing. In 1947, girls scored higher than boys in spelling, language, clerical speed and accuracy, and verbal ability. The boys outpaced the girls in mechanical, verbal, and abstract reasoning, space relations, and numerical ability. By 1980, the only difference remaining was a gap in math performance in the later years of high school, and that's disappearing.

↦ **Women do "men's work."** The separation between women's work and men's is narrowing, too. Women have more job options than ever before: We're now fire fighters, telephone repair people, carpenters, pipe fitters, police officers. Women are construction workers—in fact, there are over 94,000 women-owned construction firms in the United States. Today, nearly half of all medical students are women.

↦ **Some attitudes are changing.** Overall, women make up about 46 percent of the workforce, according to the *Statistical Bulletin of the Metropolitan Life Insurance Company* (July 1994). Yet 60 percent of women in professional positions have jobs in "traditional" female occupations such as nursing or teaching. And even though a 1982 poll of more than 1,000 adults for the National Opinion Research Center's General Social Survey found an 82 percent willingness to let women be truck mechanics, in a 1989 Roper Center poll, 37 percent of 1,473 adults think that jobs requiring heavy lifting or hard labor should be off-limits to women. The 1989 poll, however, did find also that 79 percent of respondents felt women should be allowed to be fire fighters or police officers; 80 percent said women should have a chance to do construction jobs.

"Nowadays, there should be no such thing as 'women's jobs' and 'men's jobs,' " says Arleen Winfield, a social science adviser with the Women's Bureau, a part of the U.S. Department of Labor that sets standards and makes policy on issues of interest to wage-earning women. "In addition to laws in their favor, women need to know their rights and how to exercise them." Entrance into apprenticeship programs is based on tests and interviews, and women cannot be excluded from federally registered programs on the basis of sex. In 1993 women made up just over 10 percent of skilled tradesworkers—so there's room for improvement.

How to Use the Truth

To give girls and women a fair shot at opportunities in mathematical, scientific, and mechanical careers, and to give boys a more accurate view of female abilities:

↔ **Push.** "A number of studies say that girls are twice as likely to be allowed to drop a higher-level math or science course," says Rosalie Hydock-Sauck, a Scottsdale, Arizona, consultant who conducts gender-equity training. Encourage a girl to take four years of high-school math by explaining that it will expand her career options later.

↔ **Encourage some all-girl activities.** Many teenage girls worry that if they appear too smart or competent, boys will be turned off. So encourage girls to be themselves around boys, or nothing will change. Also provide some single-sex activities, too, so she can have practice performing at her best without worrying about disapproval from the boys. The Girl Scouts now offer a reward for technical achievement, a new computer badge.

↔ **Encourage independence.** Let her choose some volunteer work or other after-school activity. She can find out if she has mechanical or mathematical skills and learn from people other than her family how valuable she is.

↔ **Encourage her plans.** Help a young girl concentrate on her schoolwork and non-traditional career planning—ideally, this should begin around the seventh grade. Be careful not to value a girl only on appearance or popularity.

↔ **Find models.** More and more mothers are making sure that the girls and women their children read about are strong and smart. This is why the *Madeline* series is so popular. Says writer Anna Quindlen in the introduction to one collection of *Madeline* stories, "She is utterly fearless and sure of herself, small in stature but large in moxie. Not afraid of mice, of ice, or of teetering on a stone bridge over a river."

With children we can also discuss women passed over in history and literature who have made significant contributions. Finally, we can make sure girls (and boys) see women being doctors, astronauts, and plumbers, and men being nurses, secretaries, and homemakers.

↪ *Be a model.* If you're a woman engineer, scientist, or mathematician, let girls see you at work.

↪ *Be a handy mom.* If you're a mother who's not a mechanical wizard yet but want to show your children that women *can* be, here's how to start:

—Fix something with glue.

—Buy and personalize a toolbox (with tools).

—Learn to operate a computer.

—Memorize the parts of the car under the hood and know what they do. Check the oil.

—Change a blown fuse.

—Make a habit of troubleshooting any mechanical problem before calling in the nearest man.

Then move to a higher level:

—Build something with nails, screws, or bolts.

—Set up a personal workbench where broken items can be fixed.

—Change the oil in the car. Change a tire.

—Buy a kit for a radio or some other machine and assemble the item by following the directions.

—Take a course in math, physics, or a practical trade.

—Invent something.

—Let your children see you doing any of the above.

↪ *Create opportunities.* Through the P.T.A. or science department in your local school, suggest and help set up an invention convention and encourage girls to participate. Students first submit plans for a device or process; then the best ones are selected to be produced or created.

↪ *Feminize the library.* Make sure public and school libraries have up-to-date materials detailing women's accomplishments. Donate a book about women inventors; make sure the card catalog or electronic database includes references to women when you check specific topics.

↦ ***Activate the bias detector.*** Watch for instances in books, films, and other media where girls or women are stereotyped as helpless, weak, or dumb. Correct the inappropriate image or find a substitute.

↦ ***Check up.*** We can read the books children are reading, find out what happens in class, ask what the guidance counselor said. If we're not satisfied, we can get involved.

↦ ***Complain.*** A well-written letter may help someone realize that he or she has been unfair. If you don't want to take on the system alone, you can try forming a group of interested people. Sexism in books, movies, and television—all stereotyping creates lasting impressions on children. Let's be the generation that gives women a mechanical advantage.

COUNTERING THE MYTH THAT WOMEN ARE NOT MECHANICAL

Men and women together can defeat the myth that women aren't mechanical. We need to:

Object. Speak out when we see girls and women being treated as if they have no mechanical or math ability. Girls and women who hear this often enough begin to believe it's true.

Correct. Whenever possible, try to correct unfair situations, not just walk away from them. Make sure women get due credit for their products, repairs, and skills at work and at home.

Reject. Reject the urge to automatically refer all mechanical and mathematical tasks to men. If you're not mechanical or mathematical, it's as a *person*, not as a *woman*, that you need help.

Respect. Give girls and women who have succeeded in science the respect they deserve.

CHAPTER 8

The Myth:

"Mothers make kids neurotic"

The Myth:

- Mothers are at fault if a child is shy . . .
- Or too sensitive . . .
- Or too messy or too neat . . .
- Or spoiled.
- Mothers can make an infant calm or colicky.
- Mothers can confuse a child by talking to him or her in "baby talk."
- Mothers overfeed children and make them fat or anorexic.
- Working mothers have children with problems.

Who Believes It?

If a child is neurotic, is it the mother's fault?

Even though the non-computer-based local surveys predicted most people would say yes and identified this as one of the fourteen most frequently heard gender stereotypes, women who participated in the PRODIGY Poll don't buy into it. Among married women who took part in the poll, a whopping 86 percent of them reject this idea. So do 84 percent of divorced and separated women, and 78 percent of single women.

And I'm happy to report that most men also reject the statement, too. But about one in four men still does believe the myth to be true: 25 percent of the married men, 27 percent of single men, and 29 percent of the divorced and separated men believe mothers make kids neurotic.

The numbers remain about the same for men and women no matter how old they are, and a man or woman's occupation doesn't seem to affect their belief system on this one, either.

So the good news is that we women are saying we don't believe we make our children neurotic. The bad news is that one in four husbands, fathers, and sons still does, and probably blame us for our offspring's anxieties, phobias, shyness, or depression. In addition, although women say they don't believe they make their children neurotic, they do say they tend to feel guilty if their children have problems! Listen to some of the quotes from the non-computer-based survey and interviews:

Male, age fifty-four: "It's a shared responsibility. Fathers have a tendency to be more exacting and demanding, so they create trauma, too."

Female, age twenty-four: "Some mothers do give their children a problem because they don't let go."

Male, age fifty-three: "My mother brought up six kids without ever raising her voice. So I know women can be great mothers!"

Female, age forty-two: "I feel everything that's wrong with my son is my fault . . . even his poor vision. Maybe it's my genetics or a pregnancy problem."

Female, age thirty-six: "My baby is only two weeks old, and I don't even know if I should pick her up when she cries or let her learn to put herself to sleep. Of course I worry about traumatizing her."

Male, age thirty-two: "Even though the mother spends more time with the kid than the father, that doesn't mean she's all to blame. Fathers hurt children by not being there."

Female, age sixty-two: "I always blamed my mother for my shyness. Now I realize that my own son's outgoing, and I can't take the credit. If mothers don't get the credit, they don't get the blame either."

The Truth

Women give birth, sometimes breast-feed, and usually change most of the diapers. We praise, we discipline, and we generally spend more time with children than anyone else in the family or outside of it. American children spend an average of ten hours a day alone with mothers, compared with less than one hour (0.7 hour) a day with fathers, according to a survey by the High/Scope Educational Research Foundation in Ypsilanti, Michigan.

Mothers influence their children—of course!—but a child is not a tabula rasa (blank slate). Anyone who has had two or more children knows how different babies' temperaments can be from the day they are born. Common sense says it's unlikely that mothers could have shaped them so early, and research is now beginning to say much the same. Aspects of personality styles, much of temperament, many kinds of mental illness, and even some behaviors for which mothers have traditionally been blamed turn out to be part heredity, peer influence, or Dad, too.

↔ **Heredity influences temperament.** According to researchers at the University of Maryland in 1994, brain-wave activity of infants and toddlers can be mapped and the patterns can be used to predict the type of temperament an infant will develop: cautious and reserved, or adventurous and uninhibited. And fussy, fidgety babies, the researchers found, show an identifiable brain-wave pattern.

From the University of Wisconsin in Madison comes research with 700 sets of twins showing that traits including fear, shyness, and distress are more influenced by inherited genetic characteristics than by experience or parenting. A significant number of people are just born that way, concludes behavioral geneticist H. Hill Goldsmith, quoted in the *Los Angeles Times*: "Forty to 60 percent of many personality characteristics seem to be genetic . . . but [they can] be modified over a lifetime." Boys, for example, shed innate fearfulness more often than girls—perhaps in response to social pressure, he points out.

➻ *Heredity contributes to shyness.* Early-developing shyness is probably the result of an overly sensitive nervous system marked by blushing, shaking, sweating, or crying, find Wake Forest University experts. Other biological psychiatry studies at the University of Arizona find this type of nervous system is also linked to a lower tolerance for pain, nasal allergies, and chemical sensitivities.

In new research on 300 infants, Harvard University psychologist Jerome Kagan, Ph.D., found a genetic component for shy and inhibited children, which he reported at the annual meeting of the American Association for the Advancement of Science on February 19, 1994. One baby in five is born with a genetic tendency to shyness, and 60 percent will probably continue to be that way through school. The *Los Angeles Times* quoted Dr. Kagan: "There are many American parents who blame themselves when they have a five-year-old child who is timid or shy . . . [now] a sizable burden of guilt is lifted."

➻ *Heredity influences some behavior.* When psychologist Thomas J. Bouchard, Jr., Ph.D., professor of psychology at the University of Minnesota and director of the famous twin study there, polled identical twins who had been separated when young and raised apart, he found striking similarities in their scores on measures of leadership ability, traditionalism, and irritability. In fact, they were more like each other in these three ways than like the families that raised them.

Here's how twin research works. Identical twins (MZ, or monozygotic) result from the splitting of a single fertilized egg and are therefore genetic duplicates, sharing 100 percent of their genes. Fraternal twins (DZ, or dizygotic) come from two eggs, each fertilized by a different sperm, and they share, on average, only 50 percent of their genes, like any other pair of siblings. Therefore, a trait that turns up more often in both members of an identical (MZ) pair than it does in both members of a DZ pair is likely to have some basis in the genes. If both twins possess a trait, they are said to be "concordant." If they are not, they are "discordant."

➻ *Heredity influences mental health.* By comparing fraternal twins with identical twins, a study of 1,566 twins from the Medical College of Virginia found that genetics accounts for about *half* the risk of **depression.**

The same study finds a genetic component to the susceptibility to **nicotine addiction,** too. Heredity may influence how nervous system receptors react to the nicotine, says study leader Kenneth Kendler, M.D.

The risk of suffering **manic depression** (also known as **bipolar illness**) was linked to genetics by researchers at Thomas Jefferson University in 1994. **Panic attacks,** previously thought to be the result of nervous parenting, are biochemical events triggered by blood chemistry changes resulting from hyperventilation, as we mentioned in Chapter Six. If an identical twin suffers from panic attacks, 31 percent of the co-twins do also, but among fraternal twins there is no concordance. In addition, the 1993 World Congress on Psychiatric Genetics focused on family, twin, and adoption studies, and reported that psychiatric disorders such as schizophrenia, manic depression, autism, substance abuse, and attention deficit hyperactivity disorder do have a genetic component.

Studies of twins and of alcohol-dependent patients point to an inherited vulnerability to **alcohol dependence,** too. National Institute on Alcohol Abuse and Alcoholism director Enoch Gordis, M.D., reports that genetics influences alcohol-seeking behavior, acute sensitivity, rate at which alcohol is metabolized, chronic tolerance, physical dependence, and susceptibility to withdrawal seizures.

Clearly, there is not just one single gene at the root of alcoholism, but the Institute's Collaborative Study of the Genetics of Alcoholism (COGA) looked at 800 individuals from alcoholic families and revealed that exposure to alcohol induces both acute and chronic changes in levels of a variety of neurotransmitters involved in the sensation of reward, especially in vulnerable individuals.

And a study of more than 1,000 female twin pairs by the Medical College of Virginia concluded that genes contribute substantially to the risk of a woman's developing problems with alcohol. Researchers say that's about the same as the alcoholism risk for men, a little higher than the genetic risk for major depression, and a little lower than the risk for schizophrenia and bipolar disease in the already-at-risk population.

But how do these studies explain identical twins who are not identical for alcoholism? The researchers speculate that the twins who did not develop alcoholism probably didn't share some environmental triggers. This hypothesis rules out a relationship between alcoholism and *parental* use of alcohol, because both twins shared that experience!

Schizophrenia was once blamed on the "schizophrenogenic" ("schizophrenia-producing") mother, but this type of psychosis now seems to be generated more by nature than by nurture. In 1989, Irving I. Gottesman, Ph.D., a University of Virginia researcher who pioneered genetic research on schizophrenia, found that children of a nonschizophrenic identical twin (MZ) develop schizophrenia at the same rate as their cousins whose parent is a schizophrenic twin, suggesting that being raised by a normal parent does not necessarily protect a child from the disorder if he or she has predisposing genes.

Monte Buchsbaum, M.D., at the Mount Sinai School of Medicine in New York City, used new scanning technologies—electroencephalographs (EEGs), positron emission tomography (PET scans), and X-ray computed tomography—and found that schizophrenics' brain metabolism is abnormal. Studies among twins and non-twins show that, compared with nonschizophrenics, many schizophrenics demonstrate markedly reduced cerebral blood flow and metabolic rate in the brain site of many cognitive processes.

Like alcoholism, schizophrenia may have a genetic component, but both identical twins don't always develop the problem because of environmental differences. But environment is more than where one grew up, parents' marital status, or toilet training. It can also be a physical or biological environment or peer relationships, school experiences, and, later, differences in marital and occupational experiences . . . so parents need not jump to self-blame.

↔ *Genes influence personality.* We all know our genes determine physical appearance, such as eye color and hair texture. Research in the last fifteen years has found that our genes may also direct a good deal of how we act. Traits that seem influenced by our genes include extroversion (sociability), neuroticism (emotional instability), dominance, aggressiveness, and even how we speak and gesture. Harvard psychologist Jerome Kagan says that at least 150 different chemicals determine how our brain's neurons will fire, and our body chemistry is dictated by our genes. The resulting patterns of thresholds, abilities, sensitivities, and problems may be as personal as our fingerprints. Current consensus is that nature and nurture have about an equal share in personality traits like achievement motivation, conscientiousness, and conservatism.

↦ *Eating behavior is not all the mother's fault, either.* A Danish study of 540 adopted children found eating behavior and weight are also somewhat predetermined. Children's weight correlated with the weight of their genetic (biological) parents, but had *no* correlation with the weight of their adoptive parents or the adoptive mother who fed them and ate with them.

↦ *Children of working mothers do fine.* In a 1994 Gallup Poll of 1,000 women, eight out of ten working mothers said they are extremely or very satisfied with how well their children were doing, and 90 percent of mothers said their children are happy. Children may even do *better* with working mothers, as long as the parent likes her job and isn't putting in extreme overtime hours. An Ohio State study of almost 600 mothers and their children found that the effects of a mother's job on her young children depend mainly on her job satisfaction. If a mother finds her work challenging and complex, she's energized and interacts with her children that way.

↦ *Baby talk is fine.* Fathers often warn mothers that baby-talking can retard a child's language development. But I have good news for all of you who do it anyway. It seems that baby talk is a natural response that babies elicit from adults! It's called child-directed speech, and it stimulates more smiles and babbling than adult speech, readies children for understanding other children, and actually encourages speech. You see, baby talk is always one step ahead of the child's talk (for example, when the child starts using two-word sentences, adults automatically graduate to full sentences and pull the child's development along). So if you do it, enjoy it. Just don't forget to drop it when you're talking to adults!

↦ *Fathers share the responsibility.* It's not only inaccurate to say mothers "create" their children's problems, it's outdated and sexist. When there is an influence, fathers today are often as great an influence!

Fathers were the primary caregivers for 15 percent of all preschoolers in 1988, and 20 percent of primary caregivers—or 2 million—were at-home dads in 1991, according to the U.S. Bureau of the Census. Long-term unemployment by men and the high cost of child care are among the most frequently cited reasons for the increase.

Fathers today are also more involved in their wives' pregnancies, childbirth, and in the early care of their children than their fathers were, although more disappear (after divorce) than in previous generations. A *Redbook* survey found that 85 percent of married men expect to be present at the births of their children. Few of these men had their fathers present at their own births.

The same survey of more than 400 fathers ranging in age from eighteen to seventy-nine found 86 percent also say they have taken their child to the doctor, and 54 percent agree that men, in general, are as good at child-rearing as women.

How to Use the Truth

Although mothers have to share some responsibility with fathers for how their children turn out, mothers (and fathers) don't really "create" their children. Heredity provides susceptibilities, capabilities, tendencies, and vulnerabilities. And parenthood does provide opportunities to help children help themselves:

↪ *Get to know your children.* Notice how they affect others, and you, too, because their temperament probably influenced *your* reactions to them from the day they were born—as much as (if not more than) your personality influenced *their* development. Getting to know them, however, is difficult if you're busy taking all the blame or credit for their personality and style. So refocus on them. Provide an environment of learning and support that helps them know themselves, overcome barriers, and develop potentials.

↪ *Encourage the positive.* We tend to notice when they're naughty, and scold, but we sometimes forget to notice the good, too, and reward it. When a child is compassionate, say how nice it is to see that. When a child cleans up her mess, thank her. Spell out the good behavior you do want, and when you get it, give feedback. You're more likely to get it again. And you taught good manners by example.

↦ ***Help shy children.*** Shyness can lower a child's self-esteem by interfering with risk-taking, exploration, and interaction with people who build self-esteem. Since shyness seems to have a genetic component, a shy child may always feel shy inside—but he or she can learn to deal with it. You can help by encouraging shy children to rehearse critical events such as show-and-tell, not putting them on the spot, praising them when they show confidence, and *not* labeling them as "shy"—labels can act as self-fulfilling prophecies. So reread the section on managing shyness in Chapter 1, and encourage your child to go out, talk with people, and listen carefully to others.

↦ ***Help sensitive children.*** Psychologists say as many as one or two out of ten children are sensitive—they're especially empathetic and perceptive about people's behaviors and emotions, more compliant than competitive, well-behaved, prone to cry easily, and are likely to take things very personally. Experts say most sensitive people were born with that predisposition, but you can help sensitive children become a little bolder:

—Don't make them think of themselves as different or delicate by overprotecting them. Other kids will notice and tease them.

—If they become emotional in front of others, just say you understand. Later on, practice what they can say or do instead of crying.

—Finally, show them how to be more easygoing. Make some mistakes in front of them (like "accidentally" knocking over your tower of blocks with a toddler, or making a wrong turn when you're driving with an older child), then accept your error easily. Your actions are worth a thousand words.

↦ ***Deal with birth order.*** If you've wondered if birth order helps shape our personality, the data say yes. Let's start with firstborns. They're more likely to excel on the SATs, earn Ph.D.s, be listed in *Who's Who in America,* or become an astronaut or a U.S. president, probably because they get all their parents' attention and demands for a while. They learn to work hard, and seek and get approval, but they also may learn to be self-critical and driven.

To help oldest children:

—Praise their humor and personality as much as their grades.

—Try to guide them to limit the number of projects they take on.

—Encourage them to have some fun!

Now, for the middle child. Middle children make great friends or mates: They're the most likely to be monogamous, because they're loyal to people who pay attention to them, and the least likely to go into therapy, because they're used to fending for themselves. But birth-order experts also say middle children tend to feel misunderstood or left out because they'll never catch up to the older children and they're not as novel as the baby. To help their self-esteem:

—Ask their opinions, really listen to their answers, and quote them in front of the rest of the family.

—Take lots of photographs of them, because they complain they're never in the family album, and remind them often that they're unique.

And last but not least, the baby of the family. Because the babies get lots of affection but not much direct attention (parents are often tired and distracted by then), they learn to figure things out their own way. In fact, twenty-three of the twenty-eight science revolutions of the last 400 years were led by lastborns, says an MIT study. So:

—Encourage their independent ideas.

—Arrange some private time with you, without the other children.

—Try not to compare them to the others, favorably or unfavorably.

And something to remember: Even though experts find birth order counts, so do gender, spacing of siblings, social class, age of parents . . . so think of birth order as an influence, not a rule.

➻ *Understand only-children.* Parents used to think children needed a sibling to grow up normal, so being an only-child seemed to be the exception. But then couples began to wait longer before starting families and also began to worry more about money. Now there are an estimated 20 million only-children in the United States, and the trend's increasing. So for all of you who have an only-child or are thinking about it, here's a quiz. True or false?

____ Only-children are shy.
____ Only-children are lonely.
____ Only-children are neurotic.
____ Only-children are intellectual.

All of these statements are usually false. Here's why:

—Only-children are not typically shy. Their only social deficit seems to be that they don't have much practice fighting physically, but a study of 200 children finds they're better at fighting *verbally* because they've learned to fight with parents instead of siblings.

—Only-children are not typically lonely. Demographic studies say they usually have *more* friends than children from large families, and usually develop a sibling-type relationship with at least one of them.

—Only-children are not neurotic. Actually, studies find only-children are less likely to end up in therapy when they grow up, even when they're raised in a single-parent home! It's probably because they get enough undivided attention.

—Only-children are not always intellectual. Only-children *are* high achievers in school, like firstborn children, but studies say they're no more likely to be eccentric or nerdy than any other child and they're often more popular.

So, only-children are usually normal and happy, their parents have more time and money . . . what's the catch? Children say it's that they won't have a sibling for help when parents age. But siblings don't often participate in care-taking equally anyway. Parents say the catch is that they have to be careful not to be too focused on these children. So, if you have an only-child, don't do everything for him or her. Give the child the same level of responsibilities you'd give if you had many children. And don't expect too much. Try to let the child fail sometimes without your noticing too much. And try not to see your child as your only chance to be a good parent . . . it's really his or her only chance to be a child!

↪ *Help teens communicate.* Teens often say their parents don't understand them, and actually, many mothers admit they don't! We're probably never going to eliminate the generation gap completely, because a teen's job is to prepare to leave home, and many seem to think it's easier to leave angry than homesick. But family therapists do have some tips for talking to teens.

—Since their bodies are changing rapidly, don't tease them, even lovingly. You can easily say something they'll never, never forget.

—Don't minimize their problems. They don't have your perspective, and can't have it yet.

—Don't explode or sulk . . . you'll be teaching them to do that right back to you. And be careful about the insults. An Ohio State University study found that the older the child, the more the *parents* used put-downs and sarcasm.

—Don't lecture or moralize, of course. It emphasizes the gap, and it's too one-way.

—And, most important, don't take their behavior personally. If they're not talking about feelings, it's probably because they're confused or embarrassed. If they're stressed, it's probably peer pressure, grades, or job worries. And if they're daydreaming or away from home with friends more, child psychiatrists say it's probably normal—not a problem caused by you.

—So, listen to teens very carefully when they're speaking, and repeat back what you hear to let them know they're heard.

—Negotiate, instead of getting into power struggles. That raises talk to an adult conversation level and usually gets results.

—Trade car use for chores, for example, or explain that you won't feel like helping them out if they're rude to you. Dr. Haim Ginott, author of *Between Parent and Teenager*, called this "logical consequences," and teens understand it.

—And, finally, respect their privacy. If you promise not to tell something, keep your promise or renegotiate with them.

And teens, if you're reading this, you have to do your part, too:

—Explain your feelings really carefully, because parents aren't mind readers.

—Give your parents a chance to state their case, because they do care.

—And don't forget to thank them and praise them for listening . . . parents need encouragement, too.

↬ ***Don't worry too much about working.*** In most cases, a child is not jeopardized by having a working mother who doesn't dislike her work. So if you're planning to work (or do), you may want to choose a more interesting job even when the work is harder or the pay is slightly lower, if you can afford to. Or, if you're forced into a job that's monotonous or routine, try to take a quick after-work break before you hit the house. Stop for tea, read a magazine, or get some exercise. Do something to lift your mood for your children's sake.

If you're lucky enough to love your work, control the temptation to work overtime. Researchers find routine overtime by *either* parent is linked to lower scores on school tests for their children, particularly boys. And beware of too much guilt, because the more a mother loves her work, it seems, the more likely it is that she'll blame every problem her children have on her working, and spoil them to compensate. Instead, let your children visit you at work so they can picture you there when you're not home, give them all your emergency numbers so they'll feel in touch, and explain not only what you do but also why you do it. Children who understand the importance of work tend to imitate their parents and become hard workers themselves.

↔ **Prepare home-alone kids.** Latchkey kids—children who come home to an empty house every day—have some special needs. There are now more than 2 million American children between five and thirteen years old taking care of themselves completely after school because the family adults have to work, and many are alone for an hour or so. If your children are among them, I've got some information not only from experts and the law, but from home-alone children themselves.

First, guidelines for a child's readiness include:

—Their age, of course. (The New York State Family Court Act, for example, says that before six years of age, most children have an insufficient awareness of personal safety to be left alone, but they may be ready for progressively longer periods between six and ten years of age.)

But parents must also consider children's

—health

—maturity and willingness to be alone

—ability to handle the unexpected

Try them out with short absences and with the "What If" game. Ask them, What if a stranger comes to the door? What if you lose your key? Give them points for good answers and pointers when they need it.

The guidelines for *your* readiness include:

—How much you've rehearsed the children for emergencies (actual fire drills, dialing, and first-aid practice).

—How safe you've made your neighborhood. Ask at least two neighbors if they'd be willing to keep an extra key and to be called if a child is hurt.

—How clear you've been with rules. The most common ones are no having company without permission; no answering the phone without a prearranged signal, like two rings first; no use of matches, stove, or electrical equipment; no opening the door for unexpected drop-ins or strangers. And, finally:

—How safe you've made the house with smoke alarms, flashlights, and emergency telephone numbers posted clearly. And from the law's point of view, how well you've protected children from exposed wires, gas leaks, broken stairs or railings, and access to open windows, poisons, dangerous objects like guns and knives, and vicious or uncontrolled animals.

And now advice from the children themselves: 1,000 self-care children were surveyed and they say:

—They don't like to come home to a silent house, so consider leaving a radio on for them. It's a good security measure, too, because it makes the house sound occupied.

—They don't want to be ignored or teased if they say they were afraid of noises or strangers in the area, so encourage them to call a designated neighbor, older friend, or even the police instead.

—And they don't like to feel out of touch with you, so give them phone numbers and make them feel that you want to know how they're doing.

For most children who are ready, being home alone is a chance to grow in responsibility and probably watch some extra television, too.

↔ *Help sons of single mothers.* More than 85 percent of the single-parent families in America—that's 14 million families—are headed by women. And many are trying to raise sons without any male role model in the house. Can it be done? Yes. Any loving parent can raise a boy *or* girl. But it takes some extra awareness of boys' needs.

When fathers are active parents, studies show, boys tend to be more independent—probably because fathers do more rough-and-tumble play with boys than mothers and are more likely to encourage them to take risks.

So when Mother's the only one in charge, she should try to do some rough-housing when her son is young, encourage sports for him as he gets older, and guard against being overprotective.

Next, because boys who have active father figures act up less in school, according to research, single mothers may have to provide extra structure and discipline: setting up rules for curfews, household duties, and homework and following through with the logical consequences.

And because oldest sons in single-mother households frequently take over adult male responsibilities too early (act bossy with their brothers and sisters, worry about money and about their mother), experts advise making it clear that they're not responsible for the family's welfare—and make sure they know how to have some fun, too.

Now some reminders:

No matter how angry you may be at a specific man because of a divorce, desertion, or bad relationship, don't let your sons think you feel that way about all men . . . they'll take it personally. And since boys naturally seek male models, if they don't have one, experts say, find one! A relative, a friend of yours, a friend for him from an organization like the Police Athletic League. (But not a new boyfriend, of course, in case the relationship doesn't last.) And here's the good news: Boys raised by single mothers tend to be more cooperative around the house and more self-sufficient when they grow up.

↔ ***Help your children if you're dating.*** There are now almost 14 million women (only 2 million men) who are heads of single-parent households, and many of them are wondering how to mix dating with motherhood. Even though some single parents never bring dates home when the children are there, and others bring them home, have them stay, and invite them to family breakfast in the morning, most are struggling to balance their own needs with their responsibility to do what's best for their children.

So here are some suggestions:

—First, ask your children how *they* feel about your dating. That doesn't mean if they don't like it you stay home or no one comes in the house. It means they'll know you care about their feelings, and you'll have a better chance of making them more comfortable.

—But don't treat them as a confidant or friend instead of a child. Making them responsible for date approval or your sex life just makes them feel guilty when they hate your date because they secretly want you to reunite with their father. If someone has become part of your life and you've decided you want them to begin to sleep over, reassure the children that they're still your priority, and then show them it's true by sticking with their rituals, like bedtime stories or Saturday games.

—And don't forget to thank your children for their efforts and let them know that bringing a new person into your home is difficult for you, too.

↝ *Help children through sibling rivalry.* If you've tried to teach your children to be loving but they're still fighting like mortal enemies, you didn't fail, because some sibling rivalry is normal. It gives children important practice dealing with anger in relationships you can't walk out on. But expect that the smaller the age difference, the greater the rivalry, because the firstborn was young when the second one was born and had fewer coping skills. In addition, you're more tired! Also expect that siblings of the same sex usually fight more than siblings of different sexes, because they seem to need to establish that they are different. Often. Loudly!

The starting point for mothers is to remember that pediatricians see very few injuries in sibling fights. That means most of the screaming is for the parents' benefit. In fact, studies find that when parents are gone, kids get along fine! Just try to separate them as punishment! The amount of rivalry, it seems, is not related to the amount of affection children feel for *each other.* It's usually related to their competition for *your* attention.

But just because sibling rivalry is normal doesn't mean you can ignore it. Child-development experts say:

—Do set limits and explain them. For example, you may say, "I can't allow you to hurt each other, so if you hit, you'll go to your room."

—Do praise cooperation, even if it's accidental. Soon the children may see themselves as cooperative and try to live up to the label.

—But don't take sides. Treat them as a team or you're likely to

end up in the middle. If you want them to learn resolution and recon-
ciliation skills, the trick is a technique called active listening: Repeat
everything they say so they both feel heard, but neither feels like a
winner, and eventually they'll get tired of hearing themselves talk.

—Don't worry: Sibling rivalry usually drops during the teen
years (when they learn to team up against us!). By the time siblings are
sixty-five years of age, only 4 percent of them still feel rivalry.

↝ *Help stepchildren—and yourself.* There are more than 11
million remarried families in the United States, according to a report in
Family Relations . . . and some estimate that by the year 2000 there
will probably be more blended families than intact biological families!
And that means millions of stepmothers in charge of new families.
Here's what you need to know.

Young children often accept stepmothers more quickly than older
children do. Older children, particularly girls going through adoles-
cence who identify with their mothers, seem to feel more loyalty conflicts so family therapists suggest stepmothers do not try to compete
with biological mothers, and do not criticize biological mothers to their
children, even if the children do. Just say, "I'm sure she tries."

It can be harder to be a weekend stepmother than a full-time stepmother, because your role is less clear and you're continually setting
up routines all over again. So family therapists recommend you decide
on a role (like friend, relative, or co-parent) and stick to it, and establish some regular weekly rituals for just the children and you (like
picking up pizza together or an ongoing project every Sunday they're
with you). And finally, if it seems that stepfathers feel loved more frequently than stepmothers, you're right. Surveys find almost 50 percent
of stepfathers but only 18 percent of stepmothers say they feel loved by
stepchildren. That's probably because children want their original parents to remarry and blame the stepmother when they don't. And they
worry that she'll favor her biological children and blame her for the extra rules, relatives, and bedrooms to keep neat!

So ask their father to help you out! He can't demand love for you,
but he can insist on respect, delegate some authority to you, and work
with you as a team. And stepmothers, don't expect too much too soon.
(It takes up to four full years for real blending.) And don't take chil-

dren's reactions too personally. Studies find most stepchildren do come to love their stepmothers within ten years.

↔ *Help children boost their potential.* I've gotten many letters from parents asking about ways to boost their children's intelligence. Not to create little geniuses or push their children, just to get them ready for nursery school or bring out the best of their potential without making them tense. So here are some suggestions that child psychologists and pediatricians recommend.

   —Start talking to them the day they're born. Look them in the eyes, smile, vary your tones, use their name . . . and if they babble and laugh, they've learned how conversation works.

   —Then, when they begin to understand words, start reading! Read to them, read with them, read out loud in front of them . . . and don't stop even when they start to read themselves. Easy reading means easy learning, and early reading means early diagnosis and help for reading problems.

   —When they start telling their own stories, listen attentively and teach them the grammar some other time . . . in private! Shame and frustration really squash creativity.

   —But don't neglect play. That's how children develop their sensorimotor and athletic abilities . . . both important for exploring the world.

   —Don't substitute television for personal interaction. Even the best of educational TV can't answer questions.

   —When children do start school, don't confuse test scores with intelligence. A study of Fortune 500 executives found most were not high achievers in school!

↔ *Avoid sexism.* Start by assessing each of your children as people. Their temperaments were probably clear the day they were born and probably won't change much through the years. As much as there are general boy-girl differences, each child is unique. Let your child know about his or her unique qualities so he or she will not feel dismissed as acting "just like a boy" or "just like a girl."

   If your son does prefer climbing the walls to climbing the stairs, and your daughter does prefer dressing up in your clothes rather than hers, don't blame yourself. You did not necessarily fail as an enlightened mother bringing up non-sex-typed children. What you're observing may be the expression of built-in characteristics or influences beyond you.

Constructive rechanneling is fine; attempts at *totally redirecting* your son's or daughter's interests probably will not be fine. Besides, the message will seem like criticism, and therefore your success rate will probably be low. So gather information about your child, rather than forming opinions and judgments.

And although girls and boys may express themselves differently, their needs for approval are very similar. Try to give them the acceptance and esteem they need in terms they can understand as individuals. Your daughter may need a hug, your son a congratulatory handshake, or vice versa. Your son may need to talk while his sister prefers to rough-house with the dog. Enjoy each child's personality as it unfolds—and the child will be able to enjoy it, too.

↔ *Deal with unruly children.* "Your child is spoiled" is one of the worst things you can say to a mother. Since no child is born spoiled, parents know you're saying it's their fault. Try these strategies to prevent these words from ever being uttered:

—First, make all rules absolutely clear! No vague generalities like "Be good." Give specific guidance, like "Say 'thank you' after Grandma serves you" or "Never say 'shut up.' "

—Next, remember to use logical consequences if a rule is broken, like "If you don't share your toys, we'll put them away for an hour" or "If you're fresh to me, I won't feel like driving you to your friend's house."

—Finally (and here's the hard part), carry out the logical consequences so children learn about cause, effect, and self-control. Don't confuse generosity with spoiling. You can break a rule as long as you say why and stress that circumstances may not be the same next time.

By the way, yelling or even hitting doesn't work as well because children become immune, copy your behavior, and even get satisfaction out of getting your attention and getting your goat.

And if there seems to be no improvement at all, consider attention deficit hyperactivity disorder. ADHD is currently the leading psychiatric diagnosis among children, and there's much confusion about it. So let's try to sort out what it is . . . and what it isn't. First, what it is: It's an umbrella term for behavior characterized by impulsiveness and concentration difficulties so pronounced they lead to a short attention span and distractibility. These children have trouble waiting in line, yell out answers in school, and have trouble concentrating long enough to follow instructions.

Now, what it's not: ADHD is not necessarily hyperactivity, although the term is included in the diagnosis and some ADHD children are also behaviorally hyperactive. It's not mental retardation. There's no correlation between ADHD and intelligence one way or another. It's also not dyslexia—that's reading difficulties and letter reversals—although dyslexia, too, can overlap with ADHD. And most important, it's not that common! Only 3 to 5 percent of children really meet the criteria for ADHD. So have a pediatrician rule out:

- *poor hearing*
- *vision problems*
- *stress*
- *other emotional problems,* because the National Institute of Health Research says this is a biological disorder of the brain, not bad parenting!

Which brings us to an area of debate: Because it's a biological disorder, treatment usually combines medication to help the child's nervous system run at a rate that permits the child to focus, with behavior modification to help them practice concentration, and supportive therapy for the whole family. But many parents argue the medication (usually a stimulant called Ritalin) is prescribed too often and for too long. Research continues . . .

For more information, consult your pediatrician or call CHADD (Children and Adults with Attention Deficit Disorder) at (800) 233-4050. The good news is that ADHD children now have a legitimate diagnosis, so they no longer get labeled bad or underachieving . . . and their parents don't have to feel guilty anymore.

COUNTERING THE MYTH THAT MOTHERS MAKE CHILDREN NEUROTIC

Children in the same family can vary so much in temperament, behavior, and abilities from the day they're born that it's unlikely we deserve all the responsibility—or credit! To fight the myth that the mother caused it all:

Don't blame yourself. When we blame ourselves completely for the way a child turns out, we perpetuate the myth of the all-powerful mother.

Don't be blamed. If your child is a tough case, don't apologize. It may be appropriate to be sad or regretful, but don't offer yourself as a human sacrifice in the name of your child.

Do proceed with parenting. Free yourself from rehashing the past by putting energy into helping children get to know themselves, develop their potential, and manage their problems.

CHAPTER 9

The Myth:

*"Women
are the
frailer
sex"*

The Myth:

- Women suffer dramatically from premenstrual syndrome, meno-
pause, or pregnancy problems.
- Women can't compete in sports because we get hurt.
- We can't survive in the wild.
- We have less stamina and need more vitamins.
- We need our beauty rest.
- We see doctors more and complain more about aches and pains.
- We faint more easily.
- We're more prone to mental illness.

Who Believes It?

Half of all men and one out of five women (20 percent) in our computer
group say, "Yes, women are the frailer sex."

Divorced or separated men (54 percent) believe this myth a bit more than married men (52 percent) or single men (51 percent). Among women, 22 percent of those with husbands bought into the idea that the so-called "fairer sex" is also the "frailer sex." Twenty percent of single women and 18 percent of women who are now separated or divorced answered yes.

Men who make a living working with their hands tend to believe the myth more than men with desk jobs. And surprisingly, more than half of the women who work as mechanics or in repair and construction jobs (52 percent) also think that women are the frailer sex! It's the women who work as executives and in professional jobs (18 percent) or sales, support, and clerical jobs (16 percent) who believe it the least.

The local surveys make it clear that this is a common stereotype, and furthermore, men rate women as two times more hypochondriacal (though women say men are twice as hypochondriacal as they are).

The interviews went beyond the issue of physical strength. Subjects were asked if they believed women are more frail in other ways:

Female, age thirty-one: "No way, no way. My boyfriend is a baby when he gets hurt or he's sick or anything like that."

Female, age thirty-six: "Let them try to give birth! [Laughs] I sound just like my mother!"

Male, age thirty-nine: "I used to think they were frail. I've learned better. Women are tough. Have you seen them jog or work out? They can go on forever."

Male, age fifty: "That's not true anymore. Fifteen years ago I would have said yes. But women have established themselves in more professions and sports and industry . . . they've demonstrated they're not the frailer sex."

Female, age forty-three: "There's always something wrong with us. If it's not our period, it's a headache, or root canal, or cramps, or some kind of vaginal infection, or sudden ache . . . they [men] just seem to work, eat, and sleep with nothing much wrong but the flu once in a while."

Male, age fifty-seven: "There's always something wrong with them [women]. They're always at the doctor. I'm never at a doctor."

Female, age seventy-five: "I'm still here, aren't I? I've been sick, but I'm still here and my husbands aren't."

Male, age thirty-five: "Women are very strong. Mental toughness. Black women are extremely strong . . . my mother, my grandmother had to be the providers and educators and backbone of the family."

Female, age twenty-three: "Aside from muscles, we're better problem solvers. If something is wrong you always go to your mother, never to your father . . . and she always has the answers."

Male, age fifty-three: "Maybe true on the football field, but not when it comes to life battles."

The Truth

Women have been considered the frailer sex for centuries and to the untrained eye they look that way: On average, men are bigger and stronger, can loosen tight jar lids, throw a ball farther, and reach things on high shelves. They like being physically stronger, taller, faster, and braver because it makes them feel they can outrun illness, disability, and death. But does that mean men are more likely to survive? This is one of the more interesting paradoxes in the study of the sexes.

➤ *Women are less prone to disease and accidents.* Even prehistoric remains tell us women outlive men; by A.D. 300, women's life spans were five years longer, say University of Colorado scientists. Today, scientists know why. All the major killers—heart disease, lung cancer, homicide, cirrhosis of the liver, pneumonia, car accidents, and more—strike men about twice as often as women, says Deborah L. Wingard, Ph.D., an epidemiologist at the University of California at San Diego.

➤ *The female survival advantage shows up early.* Although 115 boy babies are born for every 100 girl babies, by age thirty there are equal numbers of each sex. After that, the women outnumber the men.

➤ *Women live longer.* On average women outlive men by more than six and a half years. The 1990 U.S. Census lists 28,000 women and just 7,800 men over 100 years old.

↪ *Men avoid the doctor.* A male may be less sensitive to pain, according to Ohio State University researchers' study of more than 2,000 men and women, so he may be less aware of body problems until they become serious. He is also less likely to see a doctor until the disease is farther along. (*Men's Health* magazine reports that women visit doctors about 150 percent as often as men.)

↪ *Men age faster.* Studies tell us men lose their hearing and eyesight sooner, lose the use of their legs and hands earlier, go gray faster, and have memory problems earlier in life.

↪ *Men are sexually older.* A man's sexual capacity begins to age sooner. As we described in Chapter 4, he begins to need more manual stimulation to get an erection as early as his forties; a woman's sexual function does not change much during this decade unless she goes through menopause (average age at menopause is 50.8 in the United States). By his fifties, a man's erection, once achieved, may be less rigid, less straight, less large. He produces less semen and pre-ejaculatory lubricant now—from one teaspoon every twenty-four hours to one-half teaspoon. It takes longer to reach orgasm. The climax is much less explosive than it once was. He may have his first orgasm without an erect penis, and he may need eight to twenty-four hours after an orgasm before he can have an erection again. His need or urge for ejaculation levels out during this decade to about once a week. Psychological factors can complicate what was once a simple sexual release. If the fifty-year-old man does not know that his fifty-year-old friends are going through the same changes, he may feel quite alone and afraid. And nothing can dampen an erection more quickly than fear and anxiety. A man in his fifties may also be worrying about serious health problems for the first time. If he hasn't yet developed heart conditions, cancer, ulcers, or high blood pressure or had a stroke, this may be the decade he does.

↪ *Men stutter more.* Four times as many men as women stutter.

↪ *Men are much more likely to be color-blind.* For every color-blind woman there are sixteen color-blind men!

↪ *Men get more ulcers, hernias, and back problems.*

↪ *Women take few sick days.* A study by the U.S. Navy compared more than 2,000 women and 3,000 men in supervisory positions and found gender had no significant effect on absenteeism . . . except for temporary pregnancy reassignment. Labor Department figures do show that women with children under six years old miss a higher number of work hours than other women, but this does not mean mothers of young children are sick—it may be that their children are sick . . . or performing in the school play!

↭ *PMS is not a health liability.* Premenstrual syndrome doesn't ruin most women's lives: The EDK Forecast group study we mentioned in Chapter 6 found that 59 percent of women surveyed say they recognize and deal with symptoms well, and another 10 percent have little or no trouble with them.

↭ *Menopause is not a health liability.* In a study of 15,000 women, directed by researchers at the Center for Women's Health at Columbia-Presbyterian Medical Center in New York, more than half the respondents said symptoms were *mild.*

↭ *Women deal better with loss and grief.* When a man's wife dies, he has a much higher mortality risk in the following two years than a woman who loses her husband. This may be because women have been trained to reach out for friends. In one study of 86 women recovering from breast cancer surgery or treatment, women who attended support groups were less anxious and depressed and had less pain. Four years later, all of the women who had not had support had died, while two thirds of the women in the group were alive.

↭ *Understand the myth.* How did women get a reputation for being the frailer sex? It may be because women's muscles are smaller than men's, which means less physical strength. Moreover, girls and women are considered the beauties in our society—and beauty, as everyone knows, doesn't last forever. But appearance and size have little to do with health and survival.

It may also be that women *seem* weaker because they see their physicians more often than men, are more sensitive to body changes, or because society has trained us to adopt a take-care-of-it attitude whenever illness appears in ourselves or others. According to a report in *In Health* magazine, women use more prescription and over-the-counter medicines and spend more days in bed, which may also contribute to society's picture of us as the feeble ones. Women *are* more likely than

men to suffer from arthritis, bunions, bladder infections, corns, hemor-
rhoids, migraine headaches, varicose veins, and of course menstrual
woes and menopausal symptoms such as hot flashes and night sweats,
says the same report.

But it turns out that the list of medical ills common to men—heart
attacks, strokes, some types of cancer—are more likely to be fatal. And
since *Men's Health* magazine reports that many men would rather suffer
pain than see a physician, mortality risks increase even more. Men also
smoke more, drink more, and take more life-threatening risks. Men
have twice as many fatal accidents as women do for every mile they
drive. Men are more likely to run a red light, forget to signal, or drink
and drive. And their suicide rate is two to three times higher than ours
in every age category. Women complain more; men die sooner.

How to Use the Truth

In 1953, a Gallup Poll found most Americans believed women lived
longer than men because they didn't have the same work pressure and
worries. Now 92 percent of all women work for a living at some point
in their lives, and we're still living longer. But the good news is that the
gap between male and female life spans is narrowing. Not that women
are dying sooner from the "stress" of being in the workforce, as some
pessimists predicted would happen. It turns out that women who work
outside the home are as healthy as women who don't. The gap is narrowing because *men* are living *longer*. In 1970, women outlived men by
an average of 7.6 years; now it's only about 6.8 years. Men are quitting
smoking, drinking less, and eating better—news that should please everyone. (Soon they'll be as strong as women!)

To counter the myth of female fraility:

↝ **Say what you see.** A woman's accurate assessment of a pain or
illness may sound like complaining to some, or a desire to be taken
care of. So describe your symptoms in a complete but matter-of-
fact way, and get a physician's evaluation and recommendation or
prescription.

↝ **Don't be dismissed.** Don't let anyone, including a physician, dismiss you as "just another complaining woman" if you have pain, unexplained weight loss, or other physical symptoms. Fortunately, the increase in the number of women's medical studies and practicing female physicians means an increase in understanding of women's illnesses, and male physicians have learned to be more sensitive.

↝ ***Listen to your body.*** Optimists tend to live longer, because optimists are more likely to expect to be helped, so they get treatment for potential health problems, according to research at the University of Maryland. Pessimists, on the other hand, usually fear the worst and so they try to avoid the bad news—they just don't listen to their bodies talking to them. So if you can't be optimistic, at least be businesslike and factual in health matters; schedule checkups, and you may live longer.

↝ ***Stop dieting.*** At this very moment, almost 60 percent of all women are trying to diet. But diets that bring our weight down too quickly and set us up for quick gain-backs are *making* us feel frail. You've heard this before, and I'm saying it again. Eat healthfully and wisely rather than sparingly.

The U.S. Department of Agriculture recommends six to eleven daily servings of bread, cereal, pasta, or rice; three to five servings of vegetables; two to four pieces of fruit, and no more than three ounces of meat (although nuts, beans, peas, and cereals can give you just as much protein).

If you want to control your weight, I have great news for you. Willpower is really just a set of behaviors you can practice.

—Start exercising to moderate your appetite and lift low-level depression.

—Stock the kitchen with low-calorie, low-fat foods like rice cakes, frozen fruit bars, frozen grapes (just clean them, put them in a plastic bag, and throw them in the freezer), salads, broths and many soups, sliced turkey, baked potatoes, baked apples . . . so you can eat when you're hungry and not feel deprived.

—Sit at a table every time you eat something so you can't eat on the run and then forget that you ate those calories.

—Eat slowly. It takes twenty minutes for the brain to register fullness.

—Record every morsel and calculate the fats and calories—it's very effective!

—Weigh yourself every other day so you can't fool yourself too long.

—Stay away from buffets. Appetite is renewed visually—every time you *see* a new food.

—And every time you're faced with a dessert, ask yourself if you'd rather have the dessert or ____ (fill in the blank with "slimmer thighs" or "lower cholesterol" or "visible muscles" and so forth). Make your eating a matter of real choices, not just impulsive reactions, and you'll increase your sense of control and probably decrease your weight.

↪ *Gather genetic information.* Your genes are not necessarily your destiny, but they can give you information about your positive and negative predispositions. Then do some research into your family's health history and practice preventive health care.

↪ *Pause regularly.* So many studies agree that living double-time can cut our lifetime that it's clear we have to stop to catch our breath (literally) and do it frequently.

↪ *Go to sleep.* As a nation, we are sleep deprived. And women are more deprived than men. A Gallup Poll says one in three of us has trouble falling asleep because we're worrying about what we forgot to do during the day, and then we have trouble staying asleep because we're worrying about what we have to do the next day. Then we're also more sensitive to noise and more easily awakened by light.

Men not only sleep better in general, they sleep better particularly after sex because their sleep-inducing prolactin levels go up (don't take their snoring personally).

Add to that the finding by a British team that if you sleep with a mate, half of all movements by one partner trigger movement and sleep disruption in the other partner within thirty seconds. And men moved much more often than women!

Researchers also find that, besides the fatigue that results, even one sleepless night means lowered immunity to flus and infections until the next good night's sleep. We may not start frail, but we can end up that way.

So avoid using stimulants like coffee, tea, chocolate, cola, or nicotine in the evening. Half the caffeine in a cup of coffee you had in the late afternoon will still be in your body six hours later when you try to go to sleep.

Here's what sleep centers recommend for insomnia:

—First, see a physician if it lasts more than a few days, to rule out asthma, muscle cramps, depression.

—Then get up the same time every morning no matter when you fall asleep, to keep your daily rhythms synchronized, and get up from bed if you can't fall asleep, so the bed won't be associated with sleeplessness.

Now here's what sleep centers *don't* recommend:

—Don't try too hard to sleep . . . the effort will keep you alert.

—And don't worry about it, because when you really get tired enough, your brain will start sleeping!

By the way, women complain about it more to doctors, but men's sleep deteriorates more as they age.

COUNTERING THE MYTH THAT
WOMEN ARE FRAILER THAN MEN

Men can be strong, women can be strong, *people* can be strong. Here are key words for fighting the "frailer sex" stereotype:

Train. Train yourself to be aware of medical sexism. If you feel you're being dismissed as "just another complaining woman" or are referred to a psychologist for a physical problem the doctor can't diagnose, reiterate your symptoms or find a doctor who will listen.

Complain. Women complain more; women live longer. We must be doing something right! Just make

this belief less prevalent among younger men and women . . . only 20 percent of the men and women under twenty-five years old say the myth is true. The figure climbs slightly to 26 percent between the ages of twenty-five and forty-four, and among those over forty-five years old, a bit more than one in three (37 percent) believes it.

By marital status, single women are happiest with female bosses (84 percent say they're no worse than the men they've worked for), and most divorced, separated, and married women agree (around 75 percent each), but married men have different feelings. Fifty-one percent say they believe that women aren't as good bosses. So do 48 percent of the divorced and separated men. Single men have the fewest complaints about women bosses. Fifty-eight percent say they are no worse than their male counterparts.

Now let's look at the numbers where they really count, in the workplace. Fifty-eight percent of the men who work as machinists, laborers, or handlers say a female boss is no worse than a male boss. We got a similar response from men in sales, support, or clerical jobs (57 percent). But among male executives and professionals, and among men in service occupations, the numbers begin to change. Fifty percent of them still say gender doesn't make a difference when it comes to a supervisor. The group that seems to dislike women bosses the most? Men in the craft, mechanical, repair, and construction fields. Only 43 percent say gender doesn't count.

And how do women feel about working for women? The biggest complaints here come from women who work as machinists, laborers, and handlers. Forty-five percent say women are worse bosses than men. But all the rest of the occupations, both white and blue collar, are split about 75 percent to 15 percent in favor of rejecting this stereotype.

The non-computer-based local surveys and interviews found each sex very polarized in its thinking about women and men in the workplace:

Most women said women are better at handling job supervisory "details"; most men said men handle "details" better.

Most women said women had more self-discipline when it comes to work; most men said men do.

Most women said women bosses are more "fair"; most men said male bosses are more "fair."

Most women said women are better at handling on-the-job criticism; most men said men were better at that.

Here's what some of the survey participants said:

Male, age thirty-eight: "Women are 'softies' . . . it's easier to get time off from them."

Male, age forty-eight: "Women bosses are always trying to seduce men, let their bra strap show."

Female, age twenty-two: "My boss is a woman, and she's really behind me. She is incredible."

Female, age forty-six: "I'm the boss. And I'm so much more organized and dedicated than the men who are bosses in the institute. But they're buddies."

Male, age seventy-six: "Doesn't matter. Good and bad on both sides. But I like men bosses better. Just used to it."

The Truth

Fortunately, the working world has given the working woman regular performance reviews—and it appears she's done well enough to deserve a raise! Here is her evaluation:

↔ *Female managers get higher grades* from female employees in nineteen of twenty-five categories than male managers do, according to a 1993 survey of more than 19,000 employees at nearly 100 large and small companies by Employee Relations I.Q., management consultants. Male workers liked women bosses even more, rating them higher than male bosses in twenty-three of the twenty-five categories.

↔ *Women do the job well.* On a scale of characteristics considered important in business, both male and female employees rated female supervisors more highly than male supervisors, according to the Employee Relations I.Q. poll. In addition, a study reported in *Group and Organizational Management* found female managers are bright, analytic, strong, articulate, stable, linear thinkers who work long hours. They are also self-sufficient and self-assured, and show a low need for control. And a 1989 report in *Manager* found the best women bosses were seen as neither "female" nor "male" by their employees—just as people with a blend of both types of characteristics: adaptable, conscientious, and reliable; asking advice; praising good work; knowing the job well; and telling employees where they stand.

↦ ***Women do the job.*** Female managers are seen as slightly more effective leaders, by a margin of about 2 percent, according to that ERIQ study of 19,357 employees.

↦ ***Women get respect.*** In a poll sponsored by Virginia Slims, both 55 percent of male employees and 59 percent of female employees said a manager's gender made no difference in the amount of respect he or she got from employees.

↦ ***Women can be team players.*** Female managers are about 5 percent more likely to ask for a subordinate's input, according to the 1993 ERIQ poll. As for loyalty to their employees, 29 percent of female respondents and 22 percent of male respondents in the Virginia Slims poll said that women bosses are more loyal to their employees. (Sixty percent of women and 59 percent of men said male and female bosses were equally loyal.)

↦ ***Women can be good motivators.*** Female managers are also about 15 percent more likely to give recognition for good work.

↦ ***Women can be good listeners.*** The Virginia Slims poll found that 49 percent of women and 45 percent of men think a female boss is more sensitive to employees' personal problems. And they're about 4 percent more likely to listen to what a subordinate says, according to Employee Relations I.Q.

↦ ***Women are on the job.*** More than 6.4 million women hold executive, administrative, or managerial titles, according to the Labor Department. Women constitute almost 58 percent of the total workforce, up from 45 percent in the seventies.

↦ ***Women are decisive.*** Fifty-eight percent of women and 53 percent of men said male and female bosses were equally decisive, according to the Virginia Slims poll.

↦ ***Women aren't always on the verge of leaving.*** A 1992 study of 338 women home economists by University of Washington psychologist Pepper Schwartz, Ph.D., found that 80 percent would work even if they didn't need the money, and . . .

↪ **Women can handle work and family.** An overwhelming majority—94 percent—of 1,000 employed mothers with children at home said they were managing their two jobs well. How do they do it? Thirty-nine percent say they're very organized, according to a study commissioned by *Redbook* magazine; 21 percent say their husbands chip in. Psychologists agree that even though women are paid less than men for the same work, a job can be vital to self-esteem. In fact, the woman with children who doesn't work outside the home for pay has a much higher risk of depression than the woman who does.

↪ **Women come back from the "mommy track."** Women who entered the workforce in the seventies and worked their way up to become supervisors or executives often left the career track for some time in the eighties to have children and then returned to work. But a study by Joy Schneer, associate professor of management at Rider University's College of Business Administration, and Frieda Reitman, business professor emeritus at Pace University's Lubin School of Business, found serious repercussions for women executives who step off the managerial path. They often permanently sacrifice pay and promotions. The study tells us that after an average of just 8.8 months off for "mommy" time, women who returned to work by 1987 were still earning 17 percent less in 1993 than women executives who stayed in the fast lane. The consequence? Women managers in the nineties take less time off to have children than they did ten years ago and return more quickly to their careers and jobs when they do. All in all, women stay in the workforce about thirty years; men, forty-three years.

↪ **Women bosses are accepted.** Women have proven themselves in workplace leadership. But do employees prefer them to men?

—A Gallup Poll conducted for *USA Today* and CNN in 1993 found that almost half the men polled don't care whether the boss is male or female.

—A *Sports Illustrated* poll found that only 16 percent of the men polled said they'd be bothered by a woman boss.

—A Virginia Slims survey found that when respondents were

asked whether they thought a male boss or female boss would be more honest, intelligent, decisive, competitive, well-informed on business issues, loyal to employees, and good at delegating, most said men and women bosses would be equal.

—A national 1994 Roper Center poll asked 1,019 adults, "If you were taking a new job and had your choice of a boss, would you prefer to work for a man or a woman?" and found 47 percent said, "Either; it makes no difference." Since another 16 percent said they'd prefer a woman, only 35 percent are left with a clear preference for a man.

—And a mail-in survey of 2,320 adults by *Sports Illustrated* magazine found that 65 percent of men say they'd not be bothered by a woman in the military fighting on the front lines, 71 percent would not be bothered by a woman president of the United States, and 84 percent are okay with a woman boss. (By the way, the women's responses go like this: 68 percent are okay with a woman fighting on the front lines, 79 percent are okay with a woman president, and 95 percent are okay with a woman boss.)

The truth is that both women and men can be excellent supervisors or poor ones. It's time to get rid of stereotypes. In the Virginia Slims poll, respondents said that male bosses were tougher and female bosses more sensitive to employees' personal problems. But the truth is that in these and other measures, men and women can be equal.

How to Use the Truth

We already have plenty of proof that most stereotypes about working women are false. Now we need to educate ourselves, the people we work with, and our children to the truth about women bosses.

↝ **Know yourself.** If you are a woman supervisor or work for one, start with an objective review of what goes on in your office. Some studies indicate that women often *do* manage differently from men. Alice H. Eagly, Ph.D., a Purdue University researcher who reviewed 360 studies on gender and leadership, found that women tend to be more democratic in their leadership style and proceed with more collaboration and sharing of decision making.

Other researchers, however, remained adamant that there are *few* if any gender differences in management. Whichever is true, knowing our individual management styles—and how they mesh with those of subordinates—can turn what seem to be gender conflicts into simple management differences.

Start by describing, not labeling or judging, your own style. If you are tough and achievement-oriented, don't label your behavior "pushy" or "bitchy," or fall for the label if it's put on you. When a woman manager is caring and inspiring, don't call her "touchy-feely" or even think of yourself that way. When a woman manager is interested in gathering opinions, don't let people assume she's "wishy-washy." Here is how to counter some discriminatory remarks commonly heard on the job:

—If they say you must have PMS, you can say you're angry.

—If they say you're critical, you can say you're demanding.

—If they say you can't decide, you can say you gather opinions.

—If they say you're fussy, you can say you're detail-oriented.

—If they say you're secretive, you can say you're private.

↤ ***Handle criticism.*** Most of us say we're okay with constructive criticism, but social psychologists find that's often not true. They say we're not sure how to give it, and, like men, argue, make excuses, attack back (which gets us more criticism), withdraw, or plot revenge (which blocks communication completely). So let's talk about techniques for giving and getting criticism!

First, the next time you're criticized, try to scan the criticism for any useful information about your critic, in order to reduce defensiveness . . . how she thinks, how he works. Then ask for even more details about the criticism, nod as you listen, and repeat it all back. She'll feel heard; you'll seem open, interested, and secure. Of course, after you've handled the confrontation, scan the criticism for useful information about yourself, too!

If you have to give some criticism as a boss, include the positive with the negative. If you don't show that you notice the good, no one will be motivated to correct the bad. And although I know you've heard this before, it's really important that you criticize what people *do*, not who they are. We can change our behavior, but it's much harder to change ourselves. For example, we say to a child, "Painting on the wall is bad" not "You're bad"; use the same principle for adults. Next, offer criticism when you're calm, not angry, or it will sound like a personal attack. And criticize in private, not in public, or you will humiliate when you mean to ameliorate.

➻ ***Counter harassment.*** Women supervisors can be the target of direct harassment or have to deal with the harassment of one of their employees. They may also be accused of sexual harassment against men (a survey of 17,000 federal employees found that 15 percent of males say they've been harassed at some point in time, as have 42 percent of females). If you're called on to manage direct harassment, are accused of harassment, or have to advise and protect someone you supervise, here are some things you should know:

—Sexual harassment is usually defined as any unwanted attention of a sexual nature from someone in the workplace that creates discomfort and/or interferes with the job, and it has been unlawful since 1980. The Equal Employment Opportunity Commission (EEOC) guidelines emphasize that both physical and verbal harassment are illegal, so be sensitive to looks, remarks, and pressure for dates as well as bribes, threats, and actual touching. Be aware that retaliation for sexual noncompliance is also harassment and can be less obvious. A person can be demoted, denied promotion, have leave and vacation time turned down, and receive a reduction in pay.

—If you're trying to protect yourself or a coworker from harassment, you may meet resistance. Although most large corporations have their own guidelines in place (General Electric, General Motors, IBM, and General Telephone were leaders), and although virtually all high-level management acknowledge that sexual harassment should not be tolerated, most surveys find the majority of female executives still saying that the number of harassment incidents is high, and most male executives still saying the number of incidents is exaggerated.

—Start by suggesting to your harasser that he or she might not realize how you feel . . . but if the friendly approach doesn't work, be clear about the steps you'll take next. Those steps may include:

- ***a discussion with your superior about company policy***

- *a discussion with coworkers,* which may elicit other victims, corroborating evidence, supportive witnesses, group pressure against the harasser, and so forth
- *a warning that a complaint will be filed* (or criminal charges if there has been an assault or rape)
- *an attorney's letter threatening a potential lawsuit* (under the federal Civil Rights Act or a city or state law)
- *a formal grievance within your company or union,* or a complaint filed with the Equal Employment Opportunity Commission

—To battle harassment, you have to arm yourself not only with information but with the right attitude. You must be very realistic:

- *Understand that everyone is innocent until proven guilty,* so the burden of proof is going to be on *you.*
- *Expect some isolation and alienation if the harasser is popular or powerful,* or if your coworkers are unsure about who's telling the truth.
- *Realize that most cases don't go forward* because the victim fears retribution or publicity, can't afford to be out of work while the suit progresses, fears being accused of encouraging the advances, or wants to protect his or her family from embarrassment.
- *And if you do go forward,* expect the stress symptoms of any major trauma: headaches, stomachaches, sleeplessness, and depression if the case drags on or is lost.

This discussion is not meant to discourage action against sexual harassment. Quite the contrary. Information is power. If you are arming yourself or advising someone you supervise, have your support system—legal, social, and financial—in place!

↦ *Counter discrimination.* To counter discrimination and harassment, we first must notice them. Most women can recognize an inappropriate pass by a male colleague. What's harder to see is the glass ceiling that often prevents women from being chosen to lead projects, sit on boards, or represent the company at important outside functions. In 1995, only 6 percent of corporate directors of Fortune 500 companies were women. Women still make only 70 percent of what men make for the same work. Hard work alone may not do it.

Change starts at the top. Diana Bilimoria, Ph.D., a Case Western Reserve University expert in organizational behavior, found in a study of 300 Fortune 500 firms that decision-makers—such as chief executives or board-nominating committee members—need to make sure they recognize any tendency to discriminate on the basis of sex. They should then match job descriptions with qualifications, being careful to leave a person's sex out of their consideration. Aware women and men who make these decisions will need to enlighten those who have a gender bias.

COUNTERING THE MYTH THAT WOMEN MAKE BAD BOSSES

Women can be brilliant bosses, and so can men. But unfair discrimination can keep women from the opportunity to become a boss. The right approach can give us more of a chance.

Know yourself. To turn what seem to be gender conflicts into simple management differences, make potential negatives ("pushy," "touchy-feely") into neutral descriptions or positives ("achievement-oriented," "considerate").

Handle criticism. To survive criticism without appearing defensive, analyze your critic as you listen, be attentive (or at least appear to be!), request even *more* details, and ask yourself if there's anything you *can* learn from what has been said.

Counter discrimination. To be a "good" boss, be careful to compensate by work, not gender.

CHAPTER 11

The Myth:

"Women are more romantic than men"

The Myth:

- Women care more about romance than men.
- Women fall in love sooner, faster, and harder.
- We think the man in our life isn't romantic enough; he thinks we're too romantic.
- We wouldn't consider marriage with someone we didn't love.
- We watch soaps, read romances, and go to relationship movies.
- New Year's Eve counts!
- We believe anything by candlelight.

Who Believes It?

Here's another one of those stereotypes that men and women both believe in. According to the PRODIGY Poll, 76 percent of all men say women are more romantic!

The poll also found that women tend to believe this one whether they're single (75 percent), married (77 percent), or divorced or separated (76 percent). Among men, married men believe it most (74 percent gave us a "yes" answer). Seventy percent of the single men and 68 percent of the divorced or separated men agreed.

The non-computer-based local surveys and interviewees made this stereotype one of the top five that they think Americans believe. And both women and men also believe that women are more interested in having "passion" in their lives than men, but that men are slightly more easily infatuated than women.

This was also one topic all interviewees had strong opinions about! Here are a few:

Female, age twenty one: "A few guys are really romantic . . . bring one red rose and [things] like that. But most aren't . . . like 'You want to spend time' is all you get. But that's okay with me because one red rose is their way of showing off that they're romantic, and that turns me off."

Male, age twenty: "We're very romantic. But women just want you to spend money and call it romantic."

Male, age thirty-seven: "Romantic movies are called 'women's movies'—I think that tells it all."

Female, age fifty: "We remember anniversaries . . . sounds romantic to me."

Female, age sixty: "You know, my husband's really more sentimental than me . . . I'm more practical. But he tries to hide it. I try to fake it!"

Female, age forty-one: "It depends what you mean by romantic. I think they're more fragile when it comes to love, get more devastated when they get dumped."

Male, age fifty-four: "I think men are as romantic as women, but [we] do it differently. We pick the romantic restaurant and set the scene, we pick out the gifts. We're imaginative."

Male, age thirty-four: "Women need romance more than men need romance in their lives. It's their nature."

Female, age twenty-three: "Many people think that because men won't admit it!"

Female, age twenty-two: "Most of the guys I go out with get teased by friends if they show emotion, black guys even more than white. You just don't get the response you want [from them]."

Male, age fifty-three: "It's not that women are more romantic . . . it's just that men are less romantic."

The Truth

Is a romance a women-only phenomenon? The myth would have us think so. But the truth is that men are as enthusiastic about romance as women are. Maybe even more enthusiastic, because studies say women are more likely to temper their passion with practical concerns. As one of my male colleagues put it, women seem to enjoy infatuation, romance, passion, and love—they just don't confuse them.

↔ ***Men think love is essential.*** If a potential mate has all the qualities you desire, would you marry him or her if you weren't in love? When social psychologist Zick Rubin, Ph.D., of Brandeis University posed the question to 1,000 college students, he found 65 percent of the men said no—an overwhelming vote for romance—but only 24 percent of the women said romantic love was an essential ingredient in marriage.

↔ ***Men think love conquers all.*** In the same study, men were asked to agree or disagree with this statement: "A person should marry whomever he or she loves regardless of social position or economic security." Again, more men than women endorsed the romantic ideal by answering yes.

↔ ***Men think romance is important in marriage.*** How important is it to keep romance alive in a marriage? Exactly the same percentage of men and women—97 percent—said it was either very important or fairly important, according to a poll from the Roper Center at the University of Connecticut. And a Virginia Slims poll also found that the same percentage of men and women (78 percent) think keeping romance alive in a marriage is important.

↔ ***Men believe in romance.*** According to a survey sponsored by Haägen-Dazs, more men (76 percent) than women (71 percent) say romance is alive and well.

↦ *Men suffer more.* A Yale School of Medicine study found that men were three times more likely than women to become depressed for the first time in their lives after a divorce. The male romantic response continues on through the marriage. Other reports conclude that if a marriage is on the rocks, men hold on to hope longer than women and are less likely to suggest a separation; if separation comes, they suffer more than their wives.

↦ *Men know what to do!* What's romantic? When a Bowling Green State University researcher asked men and women this question, men said holding hands, sending flowers, gifts, or cards, taking walks, slow dancing, hugging, candlelit dinners, and sitting by the fireplace, in that order. Making love was low on the list because, researchers say, respondents said sex isn't romantic—it's in its own category.

But if they *know* how to be romantic, why don't they *act* more romantic?

—Many men say they have a hard time saying romantic words and making romantic gestures. It calls for a certain softness and vulnerability that may make them uncomfortable.

—Psychologists now say romance isn't the same for men as it is for women. They say women behave practically but fantasize about romance—they enjoy a romance novel or movie. But men are more likely than women to actually throw themselves headlong into romance and be swept away. They become infatuated more easily and are more likely than women to move or marry for love, too, according to the research from Brandeis University.

↦ *Women love it, don't live it.* Women may choose to read romance novels, but we're more down-to-earth than passionate about our life's choices. For example, when asked by the *Ladies' Home Journal,* "When you first met your husband, was it love at first sight?," more than 60 percent of 614 married women said no!

So what did make them want to marry their mate? The most frequent answer (almost 40 percent) was a "shared vision" of the future. Next was that he was considered a "best friend" (almost 30 percent). Then, his sense of humor or his desire for a family. And way down the list, only 11 percent said "romantic."

Even when we *do* fall in love, the attraction for us is not the stuff of soap operas. The same survey found that almost 50 percent of all women said it was his "humor" that made them fall. And being a "best friend" and "looks" both ranked higher than "romantic." How about "being a good lover"? Lower than "romantic." Only 12 percent of women said that made the difference.

↪ ***Women don't request romance.*** The notion that we're always complaining to our mates about their lack of romance—another myth! *Worth* magazine asked 2,000 adults what they fight about with their mate, and only 9 percent said they fight about romance or their love life. Most arguments are over more mundane issues like spending or saving money, disciplining the children, helping with housework, and TV programs!

↪ ***Young women want raises, not romance.*** Single, twenty-something women are not very romantic either. A recent *Mademoiselle* magazine survey of more than 1,800 women eighteen to twenty-nine years old found:

—Fifty-eight percent would rather have a job they like than an okay boyfriend.

—Fifty-five percent would rather have a raise ($5,000) than a relationship.

—Fifty-four percent would rather have a terrific body than a relationship.

And although they may dream of "happily ever after," almost half (46 percent) said divorce is either "no big deal" or "a useful option," according to a review of the survey.

How to Use the Truth

Perhaps the most important news here is that our choice of mates is neither masochistic or blindly romantic. We are not choosing partners who hate us—surveys find we choose men we consider our "best friend." We are not choosing in the heat of infatuation. Most married women surveyed said they were not victims of love at first sight and not moved to marriage by romance. Unlike our stereotype, we are practical and realistic. But even the most logical of us have illogical moments and problems with romance.

⇥ *Know when to run and when to have fun.* Infatuation is not love. Think of infatuation as a biochemically induced, temporary, altered state of consciousness. The infatuated brain becomes flooded with painkillers called *endorphins,* a stimulant called *phenylethylamine,* an energizer called *norepinephrine,* and an antidepressant called *dopamine.* No wonder we feel high. It may be nature's way of getting us to commit and start families. But it can also get us into emotional disasters like unwanted pregnancies, one-night stands, extramarital affairs, even crimes of passion.

If you're having trouble being objective while you're in the middle of a romance, here's a guide. Answer yes or no to the following questions about the object of your romantic affections:

The "When to Run" Quiz

____ Does this person have good friendships you respect?

____ When you see the way he or she treats family, coworkers, or friends, are you pleased?

____ Do you feel comfortable when you think about introducing this person to your family, coworkers, friends? Or when you spend time all together?

____ Would you want this person as a friend if the romance didn't work?

____ Are you comfortable discussing almost anything?

Even one "no" is a caution signal and means you should take a closer look at the relationship.

⇥ *Don't confuse infatuation and love.* If you're having trouble telling infatuation and love love apart, here's another guide. Infatuation can be one-sided, but love is usually mutual. Infatuation is addictive, unrealistic, and always ends. Eventually the body's emergency system and the mind's passion become exhausted. For better or worse, infatuation ends, since it is always a *stage* of feelings, not a final state. But love is usually based on similar values and attitudes, and able to grow.

Although most women recognize that infatuation is not love, we often seem to enjoy infatuation anyway. From age eighteen to seventy-nine, interviewees in a survey I conducted for *Health* magazine some years ago and discussed in *Passions* said they became infatuated. And regardless of how the affair turned out, female respondents said that, in retrospect, being infatuated was a *positive* experience:

"It made me feel worthwhile . . ."

"It brought me up when I was down . . ."

"I became more sexually aware of myself . . ."

But whether you enjoy infatuation or not, if you find that what you're feeling is really infatuation, expect it to pass—as all intense emotions do.

↦ ***Don't confuse infatuation and aggravation.*** If you ever suspected that infatuations may be more nerve-racking for women than men, you may not be wrong. Even in these liberated times, men are still more likely to make the dates and take the initiative. They are still more likely to be the ones to propose everything from a particular restaurant to a living arrangement to marriage. Since our sense of stress increases whenever our sense of control decreases, it is easy to see how an infatuated woman may feel more vulnerable than an infatuated man.

Women spend more time waiting to get telephone calls and wondering if there will be another date. The longer we wait, the more likely we are to fear lack of interest or desertion. The more fear we feel, the more visceral are our reactions: pounding heart, shaking hands, knotted-up stomach. The more visceral reactions we notice, the more we conclude that we are in love! We say to ourselves, "If I feel *this* bad, I must really care!"

↦ ***Recognize addiction.*** Being infatuated is a lot like taking amphetamines. Both are psychotropic (mind-altering). Both produce a "high," make us feel energized, reduce our need for rest, diminish our appetite, and increase our optimism. They make us feel powerful and goal-directed, cause our heartbeats to race, raise our blood pressure, and stimulate the release of adrenaline.

But both amphetamines and infatuation have their downside. They can impair judgment, so we are likely to make unrealistic and impulsive decisions, and to try to carry them out with great energy. Both amphetamines and infatuation are associated with mood swings, and as time goes on, both can be associated with the development of suspicion, even paranoia. Withdrawal from either may be followed by depression and lethargy. Resumption of either gives a "rush" of pleasure and relief from depression. In fact, the similarities between infatuation and amphetamine use are dramatic enough to suggest that infatuation might be associated with the release of an amphetamine-type chemical in the brain. According to Michael R. Liebowitz, M.D., director of the anxiety disorders clinic at the New York State Psychiatric Institute in Manhattan, and author of *The Chemistry of Love,* the chemical is probably *phenylethylamine.* Perhaps, suggests Dr. Liebowitz and his associate, Donald Klein, M.D., that's why people who experience romantic affairs with great highs and lows crave chocolate, which contains high levels of phenylethylamine, during their low periods.

↦ *Getting over the addiction.*

—Make them "just a person." You gave them power over you; you can withdraw it again.

—Get "real." Know who your "crush" really is, rather than who you think he seems to be.

—Get a life. It's a common expression and an excellent prescription. Don't wait for your next infatuation—take that vacation, redecorate, and make plans with friends. Eat cookies in bed, too. . . .

↦ *What men want.* Infatuation may not last forever, but it can become something deeper. Here's how *men* think we can make a relationship even better:

—Men (66 percent) want us to initiate lovemaking more often, according to a 1993 *Redbook* survey.

—Men say they think it's appropriate for us to send flowers, too, according to an FTD poll.

—Many men say they need an exclusive, caring relationship, according to the *Parade* sex survey.

—Men don't think looks are everything, according to our interviews.

↦ *What women want.* Now, here's how *women* think men can make a relationship better—the next time the man in your life asks you what women really want from men, read him this list.

—Take us away, take us out. A Hilton survey finds that a surprise weekend away is our first choice (almost 40 percent), and next is dinner out (26 percent).

—Send flowers. If you're going to spend money on a romantic

gesture, forget the perfume unless you know our brand, and forget about the lingerie—we'd rather choose our own, according to the polls. A *Ladies' Home Journal* poll on the subject found we'd prefer two dozen roses (almost 20 percent). I suspect roses rank high because they are so perishable and expensive we think only someone in love would send them!

—Communicate. When we're feeling low, having someone who listens to us means more than romantic attentions from our mate (Keri Confidence Report). Only 2 percent of women surveyed said they need romance to boost their self-esteem, but almost 50 percent said helping a partner with *their* problems boosted it.

—Be honest. Survey after survey says we want honesty. In fact, a *New York Times* survey found we think the women's movement helped make relationships more honest and open (72 percent).

After you've turned infatuation into love, how do you put some infatuation and romance back into a relationship?

—Go back in time. If you can't go away together, stroll down memory lane together, instead. How did first love feel? Talk about it. Laugh about it. Maybe even find it again.

—Receive all efforts graciously. Even if you don't enjoy the frilly underwear he chooses or he can't warm up to candles in the bedroom, be polite and respectful of each other's style. Find compromises. Order underwear both of you like; have candles this time and daylight the next.

—Talk about protection. The threat of AIDS has actually helped to make some relationships more romantic. Surveys say couples are waiting longer to make love, and until then, they use kindness, consideration, small gifts, and words of love to express their feelings toward each other. Men and women who are afraid to discuss sexual safety and the need for using latex condoms with each other should know that bringing up the subject is a very romantic, caring gesture.

—Take your time. Don't expect your partner to slip into "the mood" after thirty seconds of cuddling or sweet nothings. Sex therapists remind us to begin with sensual pleasures like bathing and massage, and sexual pleasures will probably follow.

—Strike a balance. The key to a successful marriage isn't romance but friendship. According to Nancy Grote, Ph.D., assistant professor of psychology at Smith College in Northampton, Massachusetts, in a study of 615 people married an average of eighteen years, friendship was the glue that bonded couples together, not sexual thrills. Dr. Grote says humor and shared activities outrank sex as important elements in marriages that last.

COUNTERING THE MYTH THAT WOMEN ARE MORE ROMANTIC

Women may enjoy romantic novels, romantic movies, and romantic interludes, but women don't often confuse them with real life. If your behavior *does* begin to resemble the stereotype of the romantic female,

Get "real." Take a look at your romance as it really is, not as you wish it to be.

Get a life. Become the center of your world again—make plans with friends, go on a vacation.

Get started. Let romance bring the extras, not the basics, to your life.

CHAPTER 12

The Myth:

*"Women
*want to
be married"*

The Myth:

- The happiest day of a woman's life is her wedding day.
- Women are taught by their mothers to trap men.
- We size up all men as husbands—if not for ourselves, then for our friends and relatives.
- Our identity is incomplete without a man.
- We'll marry an unsuitable man rather than become a spinster.
- We stay in an abusive or loveless marriage because we prefer it to being alone.
- Widows and divorcées are unhappy.
- Single women are all "still looking."

Who Believes It?

No doubt here, both sexes think women want to be married! And since part of the myth is that men are always being hunted and trapped by women, it's no surprise that men believe it even more than women. Almost 70 percent of men in our PRODIGY Poll, and 53 percent of the women, answered yes to the statement that women want to be married.

One unexpected finding was that the older you are, the more likely you are to believe women are husband hunters, even though it's the younger women who are more likely to be engaged or planning weddings. Here are the numbers: 57 percent of all men and women younger than twenty-five say women are looking for a husband. In the twenty-five-to-forty-four age group, the belief rate climbs to 61 percent. The number jumps to 69 percent among men and women over forty-five.

Single women of all ages are divided over the question; 45 percent said it's true, women want to walk down the aisle, whereas 43 percent said it's false. Married and divorced or separated women think a little differently. Fifty-five percent of them answered, "Yes, women want marriage"; 36 percent answered no. And women who have had a spouse die believe it the most (66 percent).

What we do for a living affects how we think about women and marriage. Women in construction and mechanical jobs are greater believers (59 percent), compared to about 53 percent of the women in executive, managerial, professional, and service occupations. The women most likely to answer no? Women who work as machinists, laborers, and handlers (27 percent).

Among men, there's little difference. Single, married, divorced or separated, or widowed, about 69 percent think women want to be married.

The non-computer-based local surveys show that this stereotype is held, and interview comments went like this:

Female, age twenty-one: "Women just start thinking about it earlier."

Female, age twenty-nine: "It's a maternal thing. We want to have children and we run out of time, so we want to get married . . . they don't."

Male, age thirty-five: "Yes! Most women are looking for that knight in shining armor. Men are looking for that princess but they're not in as great a rush."

Female, age twenty-three: "I don't want to get married. The old 'catch yourself a husband' days are gone. We don't go to school or take a job to find a man anymore. Now, if it happens, it happens."

Female, age thirty-two: "Men seem to be leaving marriages in a hurry, so they probably aren't as happy about being married as women are."

Female, age forty-one: "I started planning my wedding when I was four! I don't really want to get married—probably won't. I just want a wedding!"

Male, age fifty-four: "It's not true anymore. Fifteen years ago it was a ticket out of the house . . . no need or pressure to get married anymore. It's not considered sinful anymore to just live together."

The Truth

For many, the woman alone is someone who doesn't fit the "American dream." People often pressure her to explain why she hasn't married: Surely there must be someone, somewhere, who will love her or meet her high standards? Doesn't it occur to them that she may be happy? Or pleased with her life? Or prefer waiting to settling?

↝ **Women can be happy by themselves.** Many single women aged eighteen to sixty-five are secure in their marital status. A *Glamour* magazine poll found that 70 percent of the 800 women surveyed aren't concerned that they may never get married.

↝ **Being with a man isn't every woman's priority.** The *Redbook* magazine survey found that more women (29 percent) would rather relax on a beautiful tropical beach than have sex with a husband or boyfriend (9 percent). And a close 8 percent said the thing they would most enjoy is eating a piece of chocolate cake with whipped cream and hot fudge on top!

↝ **Many women are reluctant to marry.** Those women who fear that men will focus on work and hobbies may be right—a poll by the Firestone Tire and Service Centers found that only 62 percent of men agree that they love their women more than their cars.

But many women hesitate for their own reasons.

Many of my patients have said their hesitation was due to their code of honor: Their word means so much that they can't give it if there's any doubt at all, and there always is.

Choice addicts tell me there will always be another choice if I "don't," but I'll never have another choice if I "do"!

Claustrophobics say that phrases like "until death do you part" cause them to experience hyperventilation, panic attacks, and nausea.

Many say they have seen too many bad marriages and divorces even to try it themselves.

And many other women are in same-sex relationships and as committed to each other as in a marriage. The Census Bureau reports 145,130 gay and lesbian couples in the U.S.—about 1.3 male couples for every female couple.

↦ *Women get cold feet.* Caterers say it's the brides who bail out more often.

↦ *Men "need" marriage more.* In *The Janus Report on Sexual Behavior,* men were nearly twice as likely as women to associate true fulfillment with marriage.

↦ *Women's work comes first.* Again, from the *Mademoiselle* magazine survey: 58 percent of 1,800 women said they would rather have a job they like than an okay boyfriend, and 55 percent would rather have a $5,000 raise than a relationship (54 percent would even choose a great body over a relationship).

↦ *Most women don't marry to have a family.* Despite this persistent stereotype, only 13 percent of all women in a *Ladies' Home Journal* survey said they married to have a family. Almost 40 percent said they married because they found someone who saw the world the same way they did, and another 29 percent said they wanted to marry their husband because he was their "best friend."

↦ *Young women are not in a rush.* The estimated median age at first marriage was 24.5 years for women in 1993. The age has increased more than three years since 1975.

There's clearly less social pressure to marry early today. Sociologists say it's a mix of reasons:

    —broader career opportunities

    —birth control to delay or prevent childbearing

—medical advances that make pregnancy possible much later in life

—longer periods of education and more advanced degrees for women

—higher costs of living

—lowered job security for both genders

—more difficulty building a nest egg

—more leisure-time opportunities for singles

So women are marrying later, developing careers, or choosing not to marry at all.

↔ ***Older women are not in a rush.*** Twenty-five years ago, only 6.2 percent of women thirty to thirty-four had never been married, according to the U.S. Census Bureau; by 1993, the proportion of never-married females was up to about 20 percent. And only one third of women over thirty-five who are divorced ever remarry, though probably not all of them remain single by choice.

Of course, living alone is more common among the elderly, and we outlive men. All told, about 24 million Americans fifteen and older live alone, and most of them are women.

↔ ***Women aren't twisting men's arms.*** A study of 1,507 men sponsored by *Field and Stream* and *Outdoor Life* magazines found that men are not reluctant husbands at all. In fact, three fourths report that they define success as being a good parent and having a happy marriage, the study said. And a majority of them respect a man who has a successful marriage more than they respect one with a successful career (54 percent versus 45 percent).

↔ ***Many women choose to cohabit.*** The U.S. Census Bureau reports that there were 3.5 million unmarried couples living together in 1993. In 1970 there was just one unmarried couple for every 100 married couples (an estimated 523,000 couples, according to the U.S. Bureau of the Census). Today, there are six unmarried couples for every 100 married couples, most are over twenty-five, and a quarter of them are over thirty-five years old.

↔ ***Many women are single householders.*** Almost 12 percent of all white American families, 46 percent of all African-American families, and 24 percent of all Hispanic-American families are headed by a woman with no spouse present. More than one out of every two women has her own children living with her, too, according to the U.S. Bureau of the Census.

↦ **The single life suits some people well.** If they could live life over again, would single people choose to be married? In *The Janus Report,* almost 30 percent of always-single people said they would play it the same way next time around. And 25 percent of divorced people would also live the single life.

How to Use the Truth

Although the stereotype of the woman dashing for the altar with any man she can find in tow is nothing like the truth, women who *do* want to be married certainly don't need to apologize, any more than women who want to wait or skip it altogether.

↦ **Increase the odds of success.** A review of clinical reports tells us the ten most frequent communication errors that sabotage potential mates include:

1. Bringing up the past instead of dealing with the present.
2. Thinking about what you're going to say instead of listening to your partner first.
3. Focusing excessively on the negatives only.
4. Being critical about something that can't be undone, and not offering solutions when something can be undone.
5. Letting fights just happen at the wrong time instead of choosing a private time.
6. Failing to consider the other person's perspective.
7. Putting words in your partner's mouth as if you know what he or she thinks or feels.
8. Being too defensive to take advantage of feedback.
9. Ignoring the feelings behind words.
10. Using sarcasm or sulking, since both block communication.

↦ **Learn from happy couples.** If in this world of billions of people, you and your mate have found each other and fallen in love, consider this the easy part. The hard part is staying in love. So here's what we need to know from several hundred happy couples who have been together for at least fifteen years and up to sixty years. The top four reasons that couples say their relationship lasted:

1. We are best friends.
2. We laugh together and like each other.
3. We promised.
4. We agree on things.

If you look at marriage-satisfaction scores, many *divorced* couples rate their sex life, frequency of arguments, and shared time the same as couples who call themselves happily married. What I've seen in my clinical practice is that the difference between the two groups of couples (those who make it and couples who separate) is not marital satisfaction at all—but how stubborn they are about staying together and making it work!

Considering that in the nineties so much is expected of most relationships—romance, friendship, economic security—it's a wonder to many sociologists that as many as half of marriages survive! But here's the best news: The longer couples stay together, the more they tend to describe themselves as happy.

↔ *Enrich your relationship.* If you already have a good relationship, you may want to make it still better. There are relationship-enrichment programs that you can find through religious, counseling, and community centers, and though they are not suited to relationships in jeopardy because of an affair or abuse, they can help good relationships become better—if both partners are motivated.

↔ *Don't confuse cohabiting with engagement.* If you choose to live with someone rather than marry, be clear about your goals, because cohabitation doesn't increase your chances of marriage or decrease your chances of divorce. Women usually hope that living together will lead to marriage, but surveys find men are more likely to see it as going steady, as companionship plus sex, or as an alternative to marriage. Actually, almost two thirds of live-in relationships are all over within two years, and only about one in three cohabiting couples ends up married.

But does living together help spouses-to-be know each other better? The answer is probably yes. Cohabitors bicker less if they do marry and *fight less* during the breakup if they do get a divorce. And if they're *going* to marry, cohabiting couples do it sooner. But the reasons usually are more financial than romantic, or because *her* parents don't approve of the live-in arrangement! Couples that don't live together wait an average of three years to marry; cohabitors who marry usually do it in about two years.

Contrary to popular opinion, living together as a sort of trial marriage doesn't lower divorce risk. The risk is slightly *higher*, in fact, probably because couples who are open to living together are often more open to divorce, and because they've practiced being in a relationship without permanent commitment.

So if you choose cohabitation, be clear that surveys tell us that more men than women think of it as a steady Saturday-night date rather than a trial marriage . . . and perhaps that's just what you want, too.

↪ ***Know that non-marital breakups are difficult, too.*** When they break up, non-marital separations can be as traumatic as a divorce. Fifty couples who had recently ended live-in relationships were interviewed for a study, reported in *The Family* by J. Ross Eshleman, and here are the results:

—Although the majority of couples said they thought not marrying would protect them from a difficult separation if the relationship didn't work, the couples now say they had been "kidding themselves."

—The women seemed to suffer the most initially right after the separation, and then do better later.

—The men showed less emotion initially, but hung on to sad feelings longer . . . up to two years, on average.

To ease non-marital breakups:

- ***Remind yourself why you moved in in the first place.*** If it was to cut your rent bill, have company, or share chores for a while, you did achieve just that. So consider the relationship a success, not a failure.
- ***Review what you learned about living with someone else and about yourself.*** . . . This is what you take away with you for future use.

- *Review what you learned about your partner,* and let that change his image in your eyes.
- *Make use of the experience in shaping your next relationship.* Perhaps you now know cohabitation isn't for you. Or perhaps you know more about what you *do* want in a "roommate."

↦ *Consider a later love-life.* Remember the Duke University finding that 80 percent of seventy-year-olds are still interested in having a mate? This presents a major problem for women: the reduced number of available men compared to women over sixty-five years of age. There are only sixty-five men for every 100 women in that group, and two thirds of the men are already married! Many women, therefore, are willing to have nonexclusive relationships with single men, find companionship or intimacy with other women, or pleasure themselves sexually. Many others of course find their libido drops when partners aren't available, and later love-life is *not* sought.

↦ *Consider a later life of love.* If a marriage partner isn't an option, a confidant becomes essential—someone to care about you, and someone for you to care about, someone with whom you can talk and laugh. A confidant and social support buffers a woman against the losses of retirement, widowhood, moves, and deaths. Decades of research tell us that with a best friend at her side, an older woman enjoys her life.

↦ *Weigh later marriage.* Reports say many older women are reluctant to marry because doing so would be financially complicated, since older men are likely to become ill and need caretaking, or their freedom to visit grandchildren may be hampered. But the biggest problem may be less obvious. Grown children often discourage their parents from romance because they feel a parent is acting childishly, or they worry about the parent's becoming a victim of financial exploitation that will threaten their inheritance!

Nevertheless, more than 35,000 couples in which at least one of the partners is sixty-five or older get married every year and enjoy intimacy. If this is your intention, however, it may pay to deal with your children's fears before rather than after the marriage. Explain your provisions for them and for yourself. And ask for their respect rather than their blessings. Hopefully you'll get both.

COUNTERING THE MYTH THAT MOST WOMEN WANT TO BE MARRIED

Marriage is no longer the near-inevitability that it was in the past. Today marriage is a choice, and every woman has the right to choose it . . . or not. The facts are:

Married life can be fulfilling; so can *single life*.
Single life can be lonely; so can *married life*.
Both can be be very difficult.
Both can be fun.

CHAPTER 13

The Myth:

*"Women
and money
are soon
parted"*

The Myth:

- A woman with a credit card thinks she isn't really "spending money."
- Most women are compulsive shoppers.
- Most women are on an allowance.
- Wives have no idea about the family's finances.
- Women can't read a tax form.
- Women can't balance a checkbook.
- Women make bad investors.
- Women are afraid of money.
- Women don't want the responsibility that goes with financial planning.

Who Believes It?

"Do you think women and money are soon parted?" The PRODIGY Poll found that *one in four* men says yes and 80 percent of the women answer no. Only 12 percent of the women agreed with that statement (8 percent weren't sure). Compare that to 27 percent of all men who said it's true; 15 percent of the men haven't made up their minds.

But we see that the older you get, the less likely you are to believe this myth. Fifty-eight percent of men and women under twenty-five years old reject the notion, but 66 percent of men and women over forty-five years old reject it.

Women who are divorced, separated, or married reject this myth more than single women. Eighty-nine percent of the divorced and separated and 85 percent of the married said "no," but fewer (75 percent) of the single women felt the same way.

Among men, it's the married ones (62 percent) who reject the myth more than single (50 percent) and divorced or separated (57 percent) men.

Although this is a stereotype that our non-computer-based local surveys rated as frequently heard, the interviews show that many men and women reject this stereotype, with women speaking out the loudest.

Male, age fifty-four: "I'm an impulse *buyer.* I spend. Women generally just *shop* more . . . comparative-shop, take more time about it, and negotiate more. They do it right."

Male, age thirty: "Women spend more money, shop a lot more. You don't find men spending the day in shopping malls by choice."

Female, age twenty-five: "My boyfriend *loves* to spend money. . . . I just love to look, have lunch with the girls, browse. He buys."

Female, age thirty-three: "My mother saved, my father spent."

Female, age forty-seven: "A boat costs a lot more than a bottle of perfume!"

Male, age fifty-four: "The most frugal people I know are older women!"

Male, age fifty-three: "Old widows in nursing homes are conserving their own money. When women spend, it's other people's money!"

Female, fifty-one: "When men bring home the money and it doesn't buy a Cadillac, they blame the wife."

Female, age twenty-one: "Men buy sneakers every month, CD's, electronic toys. . . . Bet it adds up to more than my occasional lipstick."

The Truth

When it comes to money management, women are likely to be as involved in spending, saving, investing, and budgeting as men—often even more. Prudential-Bache estimates that 60 percent of household bills are paid by women. And our financial studies don't stop there:

↦ ***Women can pay the utility bills.*** When 3,000 women were asked who pays the gas, electric, and phone bills in the family, 46 percent said they did. In the same Virginia Slims poll, 29 percent of wives said they paid utility bills jointly with their husbands.

↦ ***Women can pay the mortgage.*** In the same study, 41 percent of wives said they paid the mortgage; 28 percent of wives said they paid the mortgage jointly.

↦ ***Women can pay the credit card bill.*** Forty-four percent of wives said they take care of the credit card bill; 29 percent said they pay jointly.

↦ ***Women are involved in family finances.*** A majority of women, 54 percent, said they plan with their husbands how much to save, invest, and spend. And 26 percent said they do it *without their husband's input.*

↦ ***Most money is spent on the home.*** When a woman does spend money, it's usually not recreational or frivolous. Most of the money women spend is on housing costs: 35 percent of our annual income goes for rent or mortgage payments and gas and electric bills. Next are transportation costs (car payments, mass transit, gas, repairs) and food . . . and it's not spent at restaurants! Every year, an average of $3,500 per family goes for food, meals, and beverages consumed at home. And an additional $1,400 goes for food and beverages at school, lunchrooms, vending machines, cafeterias, and so forth.

The U.S. Department of Commerce does list $177 billion annually spent on clothes—but that includes clothes for children and men. Women are probably labeled shop-till-they-drop spendaholics because fewer than half of all men buy their own clothing and toiletries, compared to more than four out of five women, according to a 1991 study by Maritz Marketing Research, Inc., quoted in "He Says, She Says," by Gary Belsky and Beth Kobliner, in *Money*, November 1993.

Jewelry? Thirty billion dollars—but that includes men's watches, and *their* sports expenditures are $32 billion a year!

↠ *Just as many men are impulse buyers.* A new survey by Mediamark Research in New York City finds that the percentage of men and women who describe themselves as impulse buyers is virtually identical—34 percent of both! But women tend to spend in the first few years of their careers, and men when they're older.

An Oppenheimer Management Corporation survey found the same thing. The researchers claim older women are careful about their money, perhaps because they think only a little more will come in, but older men who've been financially successful seem to find it easier to go for the large purchases, particularly cars and furnishings.

Men also earn the impulse-buyer label by leaving their shopping for the last minute. The International Mass Retail Association reports that almost 20 percent of men shop under the gun for birthday presents, Christmas gifts, and so forth, which leaves no time for comparison-shopping or bargain-hunting. Only 6 percent of women do the same thing.

↠ *Women watch their pennies.* After household and family expenses are paid, only 9.5 percent of American women can actually afford shopping as a hobby. And even though Prudential-Bache reports that 5 million wives may out-earn their husbands, the majority of women are financially strapped. In 1990, for example, the national median income for males was about $20,000, and for females, $10,000. Then, African-American women earn less than white women, and Hispanic women as a group earn less than either. Fifty percent of American working women have only $150 a month to spend on anything beyond the basic necessities. And those who have children and are heads of household have no extra money at all. So most women are not shopping recreationally.

↔ **Men trust women with money.** Despite all the jokes about women and money ("Women are magicians—they make money disappear"), a *Money* magazine survey of more than 2,400 adults found that only 20 percent think men manage money better than women. Thirty-two percent said they think women are better managers, and 48 percent said they think both manage money equally well.

↔ **Women trust themselves with money.** Surveys find women very comfortable with their own money skills.

A *Good Housekeeping* poll found that 90 percent of all women said they saw themselves as "somewhat" or "quite" competent at saving money.

A Roper poll found 57 percent of women surveyed said they had the most authority in the household for making decisions regarding how money is spent or saved. Another 18 percent shared it equally with a mate. Only 21 percent had little or no say.

And a survey conducted for Lifetime Cable Television Network found 75 percent of women but only 62 percent of men rate themselves as "good" or "excellent" money managers.

↔ **Women are practical about money.** According to a survey of 600 baby boomers by the Equitable Life Assurance Society, almost two thirds of the women but just 60 percent of the men have financial plans in place for the future.

The survey also found that more than two thirds of the female respondents but barely 50 percent of the men agreed that it's "not realistic to expect more for children than you have." Furthermore, when they look into the future, more women (60 percent) than men (47 percent) believed they "cannot expect to increase earnings every year."

And children will be happy to hear that paying for their children's college education was the women's "single greatest economic concern." For men it was providing for retirement (but even in this, slightly more women [28 percent] than men [25 percent] expressed concern).

In yet another survey, done for Investors Group, Inc., the Gallup organization found that more women than men are interested in reducing their mortgage payments. And far more women than men stay away from riskier investments.

And women are practical when it comes to big purchases, too. Light trucks and sedans are our most likely car purchases, and *EDK Forecast,* a marketing research newsletter, says that women are less likely than men to buy a luxury car even when money is no object.

↦ ***Women don't live on borrowed dimes.*** Experts say women tend to borrow only what they need, whereas men borrow what they can get. This makes women less likely to overextend financially and more likely to admit the problem. During 1993, for example, nearly twice as many single women as men signed up for help from Budget and Credit Counseling Services, a nonprofit agency in New York City. The average debt load: $3,844 for men compared with $3,108 for women. Says Counseling Services president Luther Gatling: "Men tend to sweep debt problems under the rug."

↦ ***Woman care about money.*** Although it's popular to say women are more concerned about emotional issues and self-fulfillment than money, a survey of more than 2,000 adults by *Sports Illustrated* found just as many women as men ranked money *first* when asked about subjects or issues of particular interest to them. And both listed family and sex in the next top ranks. The difference is that women ranked family *with* money and men ranked it below money.

The Virginia Slims poll of 3,000 women also found we care about money. When asked, "What would make your life better?," the most frequent answer was *money* (60 percent). The closest second was "having more control over the way things are going in my life" (28 percent), and "more leisure time" was third.

How to Use It

Women can handle money, manage money, save money, and earn money. But women, like men, can run into money problems of all kinds, too. So here are some strategies to help:

↦ ***Deal with compulsive spending.*** We throw this diagnosis around too loosely. Less than 6 or 7 percent of the population really meets the criteria for compulsive spending:

   • ***feeling* driven *to spend***

- *feeling* anxiety *when spending is impossible*
- *feeling* guilt *after spending,* but repeating the behavior anyway

These basic elements of compulsive spending are the same as those defining any compulsion—compulsive drinking or sex or gambling. That is to say, a lack of choice about the behavior, a short-lived gratification during the behavior, and then a strong sense of regret after the behavior, which doesn't prevent repetition. So if you enjoy little else, think about shopping all day, spend impulsively, and later punish yourself with self-blame or physical symptoms like a tension headache, stomachache, or sleeplessness, you may be compulsive.

There are many attempts to explain why more women than men are diagnosed as compulsive spenders. Current research suggests it may be that compulsive spending is often a symptom of depression, since far more women than men have the diagnosis of depression. And new evidence for the link between depression and compulsive spending is that antidepressants that raise the serotonin level in the brain also seem to make control of compulsive spending easier. But that doesn't mean that compulsive spenders should be automatically medicated. You can think of these serotonin-reuptake inhibiting medications as research or diagnosis tools and look to behavior modification first if you want to help yourself:

—In a small notebook you can have with you at all times, record every single penny you spend. After a week, scan it, cross-check it with your daily calendar, and look for patterns. Since you can't change what you can't see, ask someone you trust to help you look for those patterns.

Sometimes the shock of seeing what you're spending in black and white is enough to modify your behavior, but if it isn't, find substitutes for spending. If you find a pattern of shopping when you're anxious, substitute meditation, exercise, or relaxation techniques. Even if you overdo these behaviors a bit, it's less damaging to your sense of control and security than spending. If you find you shop out of boredom or a need to improve yourself, assess the cost per hour and spend the same amount on lessons or leisure instead of "goods."

—Make yourself use cash. It forces you to keep track of your spending and makes every purchase "real."

—And make yourself return all the purchases that you regret or find unneeded or unwanted! The more inconvenient you make spending, the less likely it will work for you.

In my book *Beyond Quick Fixes & Small Comforts,* I remind women who spend compulsively not to jump to the conclusion that their behavior is motivated by a self-destructive urge. It may lead to self-destructive consequences, but it probably began as an attempt to make themselves feel *better* . . . quickly, privately, and independently. The triggers for spending most frequently are feelings of:

- **Powerlessness.** A purchase is a choice you *can* make.
- **Marital dissatisfaction.** Spending can be a retaliation, a reminder to yourself that your mate is at least a good earner, or an act of defiance or compensation.
- **Loneliness.** Salespeople at least provide social interaction.
- **Low self-esteem.** If spending makes you important to salespeople, you may feel the money is worth spending.

But shopping doesn't work in the long run, because it adds new problems, like debt, to the problems that triggered the spending in the first place. So if you have a spending problem, it's time to find a better way. Let a trained mental health professional or support group help you if you find you can't do it on your own.

Now let's talk about the other side of the coin: women who make sure other people get what they need and neglect their own needs.

↔ ***Deal with inhibited spending.*** Part of every family's budget should go to each person, and that includes us. Women who don't earn money outside the home may be more apt to hesitate when it comes to spending on themselves. But calculating your worth as a psychologist, educator, decorator, nurse, and bookkeeper may help!

↔ ***Deal with money arguments.*** A major source of disagreement among one of every three couples is whether to spend or save, according to a poll for *Worth* magazine. Understanding the kinds of attitudes toward money each partner learned as a child makes compromise easier. So, before beginning negotiations or making changes, state your attitudes out loud, and listen to your mate's attitudes. This isn't about right or wrong, it's about developing a working system.

↦ *Try a new system.* If you have a joint account that isn't working because you and your partner can't agree on whether money is being rightly spent, consider a "yours, mine, and ours" arrangement. Each person contributes an equal amount to the "ours" account and keeps the rest. The common account is for common expenses like mortgages, utilities, food, health care, vacations taken together; the individual accounts are for clothing, haircuts, perhaps personal business expenses. But . . .

↦ *Know that there's no right way.* Even money experts say that there's no one system that's right for everyone, so set up a system tailored for you. Some married couples prefer to keep assets they brought into the relationship separate, and combine only those earned since the relationship began. Some divide the responsibilities: If she earns more than he, for example, she could pay the mortgage and he could pay the smaller bills. And for some it works best to put all the assets and income into one account and pay all the bills from it.

↦ *Communicate.* If you and a partner share finances, pay attention to your credit rating and don't allow a lack of communication about money to damage its status. Did we put anything in checking this week? Which bills get paid first? Ask each other these questions and make sure the answers add up, because this is the age of instant information to credit bureaus.

↦ *Set goals.* What's my ten-year plan: A larger house? College for three children? Retirement at age sixty? Long-range goals require long-range commitment, and getting there may be a matter more of discipline than of actual money. Saving just a dollar every day gives us $7,300 after twenty years of working (not including interest, which adds a big bonus).

↦ *Don't avoid money.* You may be tempted to hand over the bankbook to a mate or accountant—especially if you haven't handled finances before—or think that a woman who handles money isn't attractive. These are excuses, and inexperience is easily corrected. Bottom line: Women handle money very well if they have money to handle.

↦ *Encourage daughters to be comfortable with money.* Unlike many women in older generations, today's young women will probably have had jobs before they marry (if they do) and support themselves successfully all their lives. It is hoped that their confidence will allow them to plan, invest, start businesses, take risks, and develop a higher level of competence, which begets more confidence, and so on.

We can help by making them aware of models. Women monitor the stock market for radio, write money-management books, sit on advisory boards for financial institutions, and make millions on Wall Street. Anyone can.

COUNTERING THE MYTH OF
THE FEMALE SPENDTHRIFT

Afraid you can't handle money? We may have a different style of money management than men, but even men say they trust that style. So:

Remember the facts. Women are excellent bill payers, financial analysts, and budget watchdogs.

Give it a try. Handle a household account and then expand to a retirement fund or five-year plan.

Take a chance. Men have made colossal money but they have made colossal financial blunders, too: business failures, savings losses, and risks gone awry. So don't think your finances have to be perfect. Women deserve a chance to learn, just like men.

CHAPTER 14

The Myth:

"Women wish they were young"

The Myth:

- Women get plastic surgery, men get character.
- Women exercise to look younger, men to be more fit.
- Women march to the beat of a biological clock; men can tune it out.
- We're jealous of our daughters' youth.
- We feel useless as we get older.
- We believe men are attracted only to younger women.
- We never enjoy our own birthday parties—they're too traumatic!
- We lie about our age.

Who Believes It?

This is a stereotype that most men and women seem to agree on. Eighty-seven percent of all men and 77 percent of all women who took part in our PRODIGY Poll believe that, yes, women wish they were young. And this endorsement of the stereotype is true regardless of the age of the respondent!

Marital status makes a slight difference. Looking at women only, 87 percent of all divorced or separated women answered yes to our stereotype (if they are dating again, they may have a strong investment in looking young), and 80 percent of single women and 76 percent of married women agree.

Among men, 92 percent of the divorced or separated group gave us a yes answer, perhaps influenced by negative feelings about the "exes." The proportion of single and married men who said yes was a bit lower, but not much (87 percent).

The non-computer-based local surveys found that most women thought *men* had more difficulty with aging—probably, some interviewees said, because aging seemed to take men by surprise. Women have constant reminders—menstruation, childbirth, menopause, parental caretaking, and so forth. Men themselves, on the other hand, say they feel young until their first serious illness or until their father dies and they become the older generation.

Here are some of the comments. Notice how many women do *not* see the behavior as negative!

Female, age twenty-four: "My mother's not like that. Except she dyes her hair because she grayed early. She thinks how she feels is more important than how young she looks."

Male, age fifty-four: "Yes, they're more concerned about *appearing* young than we are. We don't go for plastic surgery as much. But we also expect more of women's appearance than ours. It doesn't handicap us to look older."

Male, age thirty-five: "It's true, but there's nothing wrong with that . . . being fit, looking young . . . I want a woman that's together like that."

Female, age forty-two: "I've already stopped telling my real age. I know it's politically incorrect to hide it, but there's still ageism in my business."

Male, age fifty-four: "Women do want to be young . . . so do I!"

Female, age twenty-two: "All my relatives wear clothes that make them look younger and hide their age. . . . I honestly don't even know how old my aunt is."

Female, age forty-one: "I feel like my age. But I think my age is very young. Now women who are seventy are just beginning to slow down."

Female, age forty-eight: "I just want my image in the mirror to match the way I feel inside."

Female, age sixty-one: "I needlepointed a pillow last year: SIXTY IS SEXY!"

The Truth

The year 1995 is the first year the baby boomers become "middle-aged," and this is the decade in which the over-sixty-five group becomes the fastest-growing segment of American society. That means aging will receive more and more of the spotlight—all the better to see how well we are handling our age.

↔ **Women accept aging.** Nearly three women in four (74 percent) believe that aging is a natural process and aren't concerned with looking young, according to a 1994 Clinique-sponsored poll of more than 1,000 women. And a *New Woman* survey of 6,000 women found that half of the women said the best part of aging is a firm sense of self. Other benefits of aging that women mentioned include being calmer and wiser (21 percent), having more time to oneself (11 percent), and being retired (8 percent).

↔ **Women can mix age and beauty.** More than three women in four (78 percent) said they just want to look the best they can for their age; according to the 1994 Clinique poll, 77 percent are happy when they look in the mirror, and only one women in three (34 percent) said she plans to do "everything" she can to stay looking young.

↔ **We don't equate youth with beauty.** Almost everyone polled said that women don't have to look young to be beautiful, and 89 percent feel fashion magazines should use models their age.

↔ **Old feels young.** The *New Woman* survey found that only 4 percent of women over fifty feel "old." Most predicted they won't feel old until they are sixty-nine or seventy-one. Even then, that's only if they have "declining health" or "lack of enthusiasm." And only 30 percent of over-fifty women tire easily, compared to 41 percent of those under thirty. Overall, women over fifty endure far fewer headaches, crying spells, and episodes of guilt than those under thirty. An overwhelming 71 percent of female respondents to the *Parade* "Sex in America" survey said they don't think of getting older as something bad. When, exactly, is old? Women in the survey came up with a mean of 72.6 years of age.

↦ ***Women no longer glorify youth.*** Women say the best age to be is almost *forty* years old, and men say closer to thirty-five, according to a 1993 nationwide survey commissioned by the Parke-Davis Pharmaceutical Company of 1,014 women and 508 men—so who's pressuring themselves more? And women feel, on the average, 5.2 years younger than their age (men, 4.7 years younger). And as women age, they report feeling relatively younger and younger. Furthermore, the older a woman gets, the younger she feels, relatively. By sixty-five years old, women feel an average of fifty-five, a difference of 10.5 years!

↦ ***Both men and women have biological clocks.*** A woman's biological clock may tick loudly, reminding us that the end of our childbearing years is approaching. But men's clocks make noise, too! The group of 1,500 men studied by the Stress Program at Mount Sinai School of Medicine saw erection decline, weight gain, and hair loss as signs of aging. But the male markers of age develop much more slowly and are more subtle than our menopause, so men's aging often takes them by surprise.

↦ ***Younger-man/older-woman matches are on the rise.*** Women in midlife are finding satisfactory relationships with younger men, especially in the year just after menopause when a woman appreciates newfound sexual freedom. "Bride older than groom" marriages rose from 15.7 percent in 1970 to 23.5 percent in 1988, according to the U.S. Department of Health and Human Services, and the trend continues.

↦ ***Most women are forthright about their age.*** Nearly 70 percent of women have never lied about their age, according to *Allure* magazine. In fact, 51 percent of women celebrate their birthdays in the office, but only a third of men do, according to an American Greetings poll.

↔ *Older women are sexy.* Women in their fifties often become more interested in sex than men. Men who don't tune in to these new needs are tuning out the chance for great intimacy and pleasure. (See Chapter 2, about midlife, and Chapter 4, about female sexuality.)

How to Use the Truth

This chapter may be filled with good news, but some of us still have work to do when it comes to shedding misconceptions about aging. Here's how to break free from our own ageism:

↔ *Enjoy changes.* With our years, like the seasons, we change. Remember *Longevity* magazine's list of aspects of health that improve, from Chapter 2: We have fewer migraines (some of us outgrow them completely at menopause), our teeth become less sensitive, we're less susceptible to scarring, our skin clears up, our allergies become milder, we're less prone to manic depression or psychosis. We go through emotional changes, too: We usually feel happier maritally, often grow more interested sexually, and become more assertive socially. And there are other benefits of aging. Researchers have found that, compared to men:

—Women have greater resistance to rheumatism, hemorrhages, many cancers, and brain disease—that is, we age with fewer fatal health risks than men.

—Since we have, typically, greater blood circulation to the brain, we have less memory loss or eyesight loss than most men do as we grow older.

—Our hands remain dexterous longer and our legs remain stronger longer.

—Statistics show that there is no "man shortage" for younger (post–baby boom) women, because they have the huge group of boomer men to select from *and* men who are younger, too. Nor for any woman willing to mate with a man her age or younger, because it's only the older men (pre–baby boom) who are scarce and getting scarcer.

—A woman's sexual capacity and interest are, in general, maintained or increased as she matures.

We can turn changes into chances to make our lives more interesting.

↦ *Be an age activist.* The more comfortable we are within ourselves, the greater the chance that we will change another person's negative ideas about aging. To be a role model for younger people, enjoy your age, tell your age, celebrate your birthdays. Don't tell demeaning jokes about the elderly or treat the elderly with disrespect. To counteract the impression men seem to have that we are almost phobic about aging, think twice before you complain to *them* about wrinkles or ask *them* if you need plastic surgery.

And if you see age discrimination where you work, don't be silent. Eventually, we can be the victims.

↦ *Look in the mirror more.* Surveys estimate we look at our reflection between seventeen times a day and forty-four minutes a day . . . but the question is, what do we see? If you look for wrinkles and imperfections, set aside time to look at your reflection nonjudgmentally. Five minutes every morning or evening just to take in the big picture. Get to know yourself as you are, not as you may wish you were. Focus on your best features and hang on to that image when you're not looking in the mirror. And always give yourself a nod of approval, a wink, or even blow yourself a kiss when you're finished looking—it's fun! My mother does it every day.

↦ *Collect compliments.* Don't assume they're untrue—studies say they're usually based on fact. Don't act embarrassed—you'll embarrass the complimenter. Don't negate them—that's rude. Do say, "Thank you."

↦ *Talk to yourself.* If you're feeling upset about your stomach, your memory, your wrinkles, rephrase your dialogue with yourself so you just describe the facts without the feelings:

—"I'm having a short-term memory problem, so I'd better write things down" is useful. "My mind is going" isn't.

—"I've gained eleven pounds and I'll take it all off in the spring" is useful. "I'm a disaster" isn't.

—"I feel younger than I look, so I'll speak to a dermatologist" is useful. "I'll never show my face in public again" isn't.

If you're really obsessive about your appearance, practice saying, "Good enough," whenever you're checking the mirror before errands, exercise, or events. Then focus on your goal or your enjoyment, at looking at the world instead of at yourself.

↔ ***Show off.*** At the first signs of aging—the slight wrinkles, the different skin texture, the gray hairs, the changing body—we may first think conceal, conceal, conceal. Soon we will realize that it isn't practical to go everywhere with a hat on our head. We can't wear a jacket all the time. And even plastic surgery can't hide all signs of age. The world will have to accept us as we are—and so will we. Besides, unlike office furniture, we aren't subject to depreciation—we increase in value.

↔ ***Don't act your chronological age.*** Most of us feel a good five years younger than we are chronologically, so behaving as young as we *feel* can energize us and keep us alert. When energy drops, the antidote is usually activity. Exercise, sports, dancing, games, and fun all signal our body that more energy is needed. Besides, researchers say your chronological age doesn't count after thirty anyway. It seems what counts after thirty is your biological age, which you can boost with a healthful diet, sunblock, and exercise; your psychological age, which you can boost with goals to keep you energized; and a support network of friends and family to keep you laughing.

COUNTERING THE MYTH THAT WOMEN WISH THEY WERE YOUNG

Since we are strong and will likely live long, we need to plan ahead for the future:

Know your financial realities. If you're not already in complete charge of your own money now, you may be one day. Find out *who* holds family resources, *what* they are, and *where* they are.

Know your preferences for lifestyles. Some women, when asked what they would like to do now that they have free time or where they would like to live now that they are retired, have no idea. They've been so busy taking care of others that they haven't had a moment to fantasize about themselves for several decades! Have fun now asking yourself what hobbies, jobs, or careers appeal to you. Think now about where you would most like to live: An apartment or a house? Up north or down south? Alone or with a companion?

It's never too early to plan ahead, since it's never too late to change your mind. Let the biological clock tick; it's a steady rhythm we can dance to!

SOURCES

CHAPTER 1

PRODIGY Poll, Jan.–Feb. 1995; 14,070 people.

"The Replens Report," Parke-Davis Pharmaceuticals, June 1993; 1,014 women.

Diana Bilimoria and Sandy Kristin Piderit, "Sexism on High: Corporate Boards," *New York Times*, Feb. 5, 1995.

"Glass Ceiling Showing Cracks with More Women on Company Boards," Indiana University, June 7, 1993.

C. Kleiman, "Pay Equality Just a Myth in High Tech," *Chicago Tribune*, Feb. 1, 1993.

"The Keri Report: Confidence and the American Woman," Westwood Pharmaceuticals, March 1988; 1,011 people.

Secret Confidence Survey, Procter & Gamble, July 1994; 500 women.

Clifford Adelman, *Lessons of a Generation: Education and Work in the Lives of the High-School Class of 1972* (San Francisco: Jossey-Bass, 1994).

Samuel S. Janus, Ph.D., and Cynthia L. Janus, M.D., *The Janus Report on Sexual Behavior* (New York: John Wiley & Sons, 1993).

Anne Roiphe, "Raising Daughters: Improving Girls' Self-esteem," *Working Woman*, April 1994.

Kristina Sauerwein, " '90s Family. Boy Trouble. Low Self-esteem," *Los Angeles Times*, Nov. 23, 1993.

American Association of University Women, "How Schools Shortchange Girls"; 3,000 boys and girls ages nine through fifteen, 1990, 1992.

K. L. Harper and W. Purkey, "Self-Concept-as-Learner in Middle Level Students," *Research in Middle Level Education*, 17:1 (Fall 1993); 400 sixth- through eighth-graders.

CHAPTER 2

PRODIGY Poll, Jan.–Feb. 1995; 14,070 people.

Clinique Truth and Beauty Survey, Aug. 1994, Clinique Laboratories; 1,001 women.

"Perspectives on Middle Age: The Vintage Years," American Board of Family Practice, Jan. 1990; 1,200 people.

Peggy Noonan, "Fifty Things That Are Better After 50," *Longevity*, Dec. 1994; reprinted from *Dayton Daily News*, Dec. 27, 1994.

Winifred B. Cutler, *Love Cycles: The Science of Intimacy* (New York: Villard Books, 1991).

Samuel S. Janus, Ph.D., and Cynthia L. Janus, M.D., *The Janus Report on Sexual Behavior* (New York: John Wiley & Sons, 1993).

Ollie Pocs, Annette Godow, and William Tolone, "Is There Sex After 40?," *Psychology Today* 1 (June 11, 1977).

"Are Depression, Menopause Linked? Many Are the Myths," *Roanoke Times & World News*, Sept. 27, 1994.

"Sex in America Today, A Comprehensive National Survey," *Parade*, Aug. 7, 1994.

E. J. Costello, "Married with Children: Predictors of Mental and Physical Health in Middle Aged Women," *Psychiatry*, 54:3 (Aug. 1991): 292–305.

N. E. Avis and S. M. McKinlay, "A Longitudinal Analysis of Women's Attitudes Toward the Menopause: Results from the Massachusetts Women's Health Study," *Maturitas* 13:1 (March 1991): 65–69. General Social Survey, National Opinion Research Center, 1993.

Gerald Klerman, *Women and Depression* (New York: Springer Publishing, 1987).

Gerald Klerman and Myrna Weissman, presentation to the American Psychiatric Association, May 20, 1995; 511 women.

Ronald Kessler, C. Foster, P. S. Webster, and J. S. House, "The Relationship Between Age and Depressive Symptoms in Two National Surveys," *Psychology and Aging* 7:1 (1992), 119–26.

Karen S. Peterson, "Midlife Marks Shift in Priorities," *USA Today*, Jan. 23, 1990.

Melinda Beck, "The New Middle Age," *Newsweek*, Dec. 7, 1992.

Winifred Gallagher, "Midlife Myths," *The Atlantic*, May 1993.

Judith Rodin, "Aging and Health: Effects of the Sense of Control," *Science* 233 (Sept. 19, 1986): 1271.

Ellen Langer and Judith Rodin, "The Effects of Choice and Enhanced Personal Responsibility for the Aged: A Field Experiment in an Institutional Setting," *Journal of Personality and Social Psychology* 34 (1976).

Cathy Perlmutter, Toby Hanlon, and Maureen Sangiorgio, "Triumph Over Menopause," *Prevention* 46:8 (Aug. 1944): 78.

Shannon Brownlee, "The Menopause Myth: Menopause Is Not As Uncomfortable As It Used to Be," *Working Woman* 8:12 (Dec. 1993): 82.

Mary C. Lennon, "Is Menopause Depressing?," *Sex Roles* 17:1–2 (July 1987): 1–16.

David Olson, *Families: What Makes Them Work* (Newbury Park, Calif.: Sage Publications, 1983).

Barbara Fitzsimmons, "Family Ties Datebook," *San Diego Union-Tribune*, June 5, 1993.

Christopher L. Hayes, *Our Turn: The Good News About Women and Divorce* (New York: Pocket Books, 1993).

Karen S. Peterson, "Divorce Needn't Leave Midlife Women Adrift," *USA Today*, Apr. 23, 1993.

William A. Davis, "Life After 50," *Boston Globe*, Apr. 1, 1993.

Mary Beth Crocker, "Doctor Disputes Menopause Myths," *Cincinnati Enquirer*, Nov. 27, 1994.

Morris Notelovitz and Diana Tonnessen, *Menopause and Midlife Health* (New York: St. Martin's Press, 1993).

Janet Cawley, "Menopause Is Hot," *Chicago Tribune*, Sept. 4, 1994.

CHAPTER 3

PRODIGY Poll, Jan.–Feb. 1995; 14,070 people.

Georgia Witkin, *The Female Stress Syndrome* (New York: Newmarket Press, 1984).

Georgia Witkin, *Quick Fixes & Small Comforts* (New York: Villard Books, 1988).

Redford B. Williams and Virginia Williams, *Anger Kills* (New York: Times Books, 1993).

S. Cohen, D. A. Tyrell, and A. P. Smith, "Psychological Stress and Susceptibility to the Common Cold," *New England Journal of Medicine* 325:9 (Aug. 1991): 654–56.

"Divorce and Illness," *Insight*, June 30, 1986.

Georgia Witkin, "A Go-Getter's Guide to Relaxation," *Health*, April 1985.

Murray A. Mittleman, "Triggers of Acute Myocardial Infarction Onset by Episodes of Anger," *Circulation* (1995) (in press).

Meyer Friedman, *Treating Type A Behavior—and Your Heart* (New York: Alfred A. Knopf, 1984).

Herbert Benson, *The Relaxation Response* (New York: Avon Books, 1975).

Bob Candor, "Stress Is Part of Modern Life But It Can Be Beaten," *Chicago Tribune*, July 14, 1994.

Linda Powell, "Psychosocial Predictions of Mortality in 83 Women with Premature Acute Myocardial Infarction," *Journal of Psychosomatic Medicine* 55:420–33 (1993).

Howard S. Friedman, Joan S. Tucker, Carol Tomlinson-Keasey, Joseph E. Schwartz, et al., "Does Childhood Personality Predict Longevity?," *Journal of Personal and Social Psychology* 65:1 (July 1993): 176–85.

Kathleen Lawler and L. A. Schmid, "A Prospective Study of Women's Health: The Effects of Stress, Hardiness, Locus of Control, Type A Behavior and Physiological Reactivity," *Women and Health* 19:1 (1992): 27–41.

E. D. Eaker, J. Pinsky, and W. P. Castelli, "Myocardial Infarction and Coronary Death Among Women: Psychosocial Predictors from a 20-Year Follow-up of Women in the Framingham Study," *American Journal of Epidemiology* 135 (1992): 854–64.

Charlyn Fargo, "Kids. Spouse. Work. House. Busy Busy Busy. Can You Stay Sane Juggling Life in the Hectic '90s?," *State Journal-Register* (Springfield, Ill.), Nov. 6, 1994.

"Does Tension Cause Hypertension?" *Consumer Reports on Health* 6:6 (June 1994): 67.

CHAPTER 4

PRODIGY Poll, Jan.–Feb. 1995; 14,070 people.

"Revlon Fire & Ice Survey on Sensuality and Self in the '90s," Revlon's Fire & Ice Fragrances, Sept. 1994; 1,007 adults.

Samuel S. Janus, Ph.D., and Cynthia L. Janus, M.D., *The Janus Report on Sexual Behavior* (New York: John Wiley & Sons, 1993).

Edward Laumann, *The Social Organization of Sexuality* (Chicago: University of Chicago Press, 1994).

Robert Michael, *Sex in America* (Boston: Little, Brown, 1994).

"Sex in America Today, A Comprehensive National Survey," *Parade*, Aug. 7, 1994.

June Reinisch, ed., *The Kinsey Institute New Report on Sex* (New York: St. Martin's Press, 1990).

Anne Moir and David Jessel, *Brain Sex* (New York: Dell, 1992).

Winifred B. Cutler, *Love Cycles: The Science of Intimacy* (New York: Villard Books, 1991).

CHAPTER 5

PRODIGY Poll, Jan.–Feb. 1995; 14,070 people.

"The Replens Report," Parke-Davis Pharmaceuticals, June 1993; 1,014 women.

"The Keri Report: Time, Nurturing and the American Woman," Bristol-Myers Squibb Company, March 1991; 1,253 people.

Robin Foyster, "Mirror Shows Men's Shear Vanity," Associated Newspapers Ltd., Sept. 7, 1993.

International Beauty Show press release, Javits Center, New York, March 12–14, 1995.

"1992 Statistics," American Society of Plastic and Reconstructive Surgeons, Inc.

"Girls in a Material Will," *Scottish Daily Record and Sunday Mail Ltd.*, Sept. 5, 1994.

"What's Normal?," *USA Today*, Apr. 26, 1995.

Jill Neimark, "The Beefcaking of America," *Psychology Today*, Nov. 1994.

National Sporting Goods Association survey, 1993; 10,000 households.

New Woman magazine survey, conducted by Yankelovich Partners, CNN broadcast, Oct. 5, 1994, 8:25 p.m. ET, transcript 954–55; 807 women, eighteen to fifty-nine years old.

Georgia Witkin, "Mirror, Mirror," *Health* (1985).

Desmond Morris, *Intimate Behavior* (New York: Vintage, 1974, 1995).

Maureen Ternus, "Temperament, Genes May Share Blame for Excess Pounds," *Environmental Nutrition*, Jan. 1994.

CHAPTER 6

PRODIGY Poll, Jan.–Feb. 1995; 14,070 people.

Sharon Begley, "Gray Matters," *Newsweek*, March 27, 1995.

Matthew Segal, "Are We Really So Bad?," *Men's Fitness*, Nov. 1993.

Charles Spielberger, *State Trait Anger Expression Inventory Research Manual* (Odessa, Fla.: Psychological Assessment Resources, Inc., 1988).

Sandra Thomas, *Women and Anger* (Springer Publishing Co., 1993).

"Brain May Control How Genders Act," *USA Today*, Jan. 27, 1995.

Bill Hendrick, "Hormones Impact Gender Differences in Depression Rates," *Atlanta Journal and Constitution*, May 10, 1995.

"Do Women Cry More in the Workplace?," *Time* magazine survey, Sept. 1986; 1,014 adults.

EDK Forecast, "Who's Plagued by PMS?," *USA Today*, undated.

Janet Shibley Hyde, *Half the Human Experience* (Lexington, Mass.: D. C. Heath, 1985).

Thomas Scaramella and Walter Brown, "Serum Testosterone and Aggression in Hockey Players," *Psychosomatic Medicine*, 40:3 (May 1978): 263.

James Dabbs et al., "Saliva Testosterone and Criminal Violence in Young Adult Prison Inmates," *Psychosomatic Medicine* 49:2 (March–April 1987): 174.

Catherine Clifford, "When Anxiety Attacks," *Redbook*, 183:1 (May 1994): 110.

Georgia Witkin, "Fightin' Words," *Health*, March 1988.

Diagnostic and Statistical Manual of Mental Disorders, 4th ed. (Washington, D.C.: American Psychiatric Association, 1994).

Jane Brody, "Personal Health," *New York Times*, Sept. 30, 1992, p. C12.

"Resources and Information on Depression," *U.S. News & World Report* 108:9 (March 5, 1990): 56.

"Is Menopause as Bad as They Say?," *Consumer Reports on Health* 6:11 (Nov. 1944): 126–28.

N. E. Avis, D. Brambilla, S. M. McKinlay, and K. Vass, "A Longitudinal Analysis of the Association Between Menopause and Depression," *Annals of Epidemiology* 3 (May 4, 1944): 214–20.

Edward Laumann, *The Social Organization of Sexuality* (Chicago: University of Chicago Press, 1994).

Robert Michael, *Sex in America* (Boston: Little, Brown, 1994).

"Sex in America Today, A Comprehensive National Survey," *Parade*, Aug. 7, 1994.

J. Meyer and B. Sobieszek, "Effect of a Child's Sex on Adult Interpretations of Its Behavior," *Developmental Psychology* 6 (1972): 42–48.

Sharon S. Brehm, *Intimate Relationships* (New York: Random House, 1985).

Joan Lippert, "Taking the Edge Off PMS," *New Woman*, March 1994.

Judith Wurtman, *Managing Your Mind and Mood Through Food* (New York: Harper & Row, 1988).

"Premenstrual Syndrome: Self-Help, New Drugs Can Ease the Monthly Misery," University of Texas Lifetime Health Letter, April 1990.

Jean Endicott, Susan Johnson, and William Keye, "Helping the Patient with PMS," *Patient Care*, Feb. 15, 1990.

"Premenstrual Syndrome: Coping with the Enigma," Mayo Clinic Nutrition Letter, March 1990.

Irene L. Goodale, Alice D. Domar, and Herbert Benson, "Alleviation of Premenstrual Syndrome Symptoms with the Relaxation Response," *Obstetrics and Gynecology* 75:4 (April 1990): 649–55.

Herbert Benson, *The Wellness Workbook* (New York: Carol Publishing Group, 1991).

CHAPTER 7

PRODIGY Poll, Jan.–Feb. 1995; 14,070 people.

Malcolm Gladwell, "Math Myth Doesn't Add Up," *Sacramento Bee*, March 17, 1993.

Alison Bass, "Women Just As Spatial As Men," *Boston Globe*, Feb. 22, 1993.

Dianne Hales, "Why Men Can't Find Things, and Other Great Mysteries Solved," *Ladies' Home Journal*, July 1994.

Storer Rowley, "Idea That Only Men Can Be Inventors Is Patently Ridiculous," *Chicago Tribune*, March 13, 1994.

Storer Rowley, "The True Mothers of Invention: Group Dedicated to Promoting Women's Efforts," *Montreal Gazette*, April 11, 1994.

Pamela Warrick, "Mothers of Invention," *Los Angeles Times*, Sept. 23, 1992.

Janet Shibley Hyde, Ph.D., *Half the Human Experience* (Lexington, Mass.: D. C. Heath, 1985).

Sue Smith-Heavenrich, "In Search of the Mothers of Invention," *Mothering*, June 22, 1994.

Doug Payne, "Mothers of Invention: Women Inventors," *EuroBusiness*, Feb. 1995.

Kathleen Green, "Should You Build a Future as a Construction Tradeswoman?," *Occupational Outlook Quarterly*, March 22, 1993.

Michael Walker, "Engendering Confidence," *News Tribune*, Jan. 12, 1994.

General Social Survey, 1982 Supplement, National Opinion Research Center, July 1983; 1,506 adults polled.

Joyce Valdez, "Girls Face Gender Bias in Classroom," *Arizona Republic*, April 13, 1993.

Bonnie Buxton, "Girls, Assertiveness and Success," *Chatelaine*, March 1994.

Ludwig Bemelmans, *Mad About Madeline* (New York: Viking, 1993).

CHAPTER 8

PRODIGY Poll, Jan.–Feb. 1995; 14,070 people.

Debora J. Bell-Dolan, Cynthia G. Last, and C. C. Strauss, "Symptoms of Anxiety Disorders in Normal Children," *Journal of the American Academy of Child and Adolescent Psychiatry* 29:5 (Sept. 1990): 759–65.

Tamara Henry, "For Child Care, Mom Is Home Alone," *USA Today*, Jan. 17, 1995.

Robert Lee Holz, "Depression May Be Tied to Genetics," *Los Angeles Times*, Feb. 20, 1994.

Georgia Witkin, *Passions* (New York: Villard Books, 1992).

Thomas Bouchard, "Genes, Environment and Personality," *Science* 264:5166 (June 1994), 1700–1701.

Deborah G. Betsworth, Thomas J. Bouchard, Catherine R. Cooper, Harold D. Grotevant, et al., "Genetic and Environmental Influences on Vocational Interests

Assessed Using Adoptive and Biological Families and Twins Reared Apart and Together," *Journal of Vocational Behavior* 44:3 (June 1994): 263–78.

Niels G. Waller, Thomas J. Bouchard, David T. Lykken, Auke Tellegen, et al., "Creativity, Heritability, Familiality: Which Word Does Not Belong?," *Psychological Inquiry* 4:3 (1993): 235–37.

David T. Lykken, Thomas J. Bouchard, M. McGue, Auke Tellegen, et al., "Heritability of Interests: A Twin Study," *Journal of Applied Psychology* 78:4 (Aug. 1993): 649–61.

Kenneth Kendler, "Smoking and Major Depression: A Causal Analysis," *Archives of General Psychiatry* 50 (1993): 36–43.

Ernest P. Noble, "The D-Sub-2 Dopamine Receptor Gene: A Review of Association Studies in Alcoholism," *Behavior Genetics* 23:2 (March 1993): 119–29.

Kenneth Kendler, "A Population-Based Twin Study of Alcoholism in Women," *Journal of the American Medical Association* 286 (1992): 1877–82; 1,000 female twins.

Maureen Ternus, "Temperament, Genes May Share the Blame for Excess Pounds," *Environmental Nutrition* 17:1 (Jan. 1994): 1.

Irving I. Gottesman and J. Shields, *Schizophrenia and Genetics: A Twin Study Vantage Point* (New York: Academic Press, 1972).

Robert Lee Holz, "Genetics, Not Parenting, Key to Temperament, Studies Say," *Los Angeles Times*, Feb. 20, 1994.

Gallup Poll re working mothers, *Working Mother*, May 1994; 1,000 women.

E. J. Costello, "Married with Children: Predictors of Mental and Physical Health in Middle-Aged Women," *Psychiatry* 54:3 (Aug. 1991): 292–305.

Lisa Genasci, "Busy As They Are," Associated Press, April 19, 1994.

Rosemary Yardley, "The Blessedly Stressed," *Greensboro* [N.C.] *News & Record*, Dec. 28, 1994.

James Morgan, "Overcoming Shyness," *Montreal Gazette*, June 27, 1993.

Haim Ginott, *Between Parent and Teenager* (New York: Avon Books, 1969).

Laura Shapiro, "Guns and Dolls," *Newsweek*, May 28, 1990.

Winifred Gallagher, "How We Become What We Are: Personality Development," *Atlantic Monthly*, Sept. 1994.

CHAPTER 9

PRODIGY Poll, Jan.–Feb. 1995; 14,070 people.

"Prehistoric Ancestors Give Clues to Female Lifespan," Medical Tribune News Service, *Toronto Star*, Sept. 27, 1994.

Deborah Wingard and Barbara Cohen, "Variations in Disease-Specific Sex Morbidity and Mortality Ratios in the United States," in G. Orey and B. Warner, eds., *Gender, Health and Longevity: Multidisciplinary Perspectives* (New York: Springer Publishing, 1990).

Edward Dolnick, "Super Women," *Health*, July–Aug. 1991.

1990 Census (Washington, D.C.: U.S. Bureau of the Census, 1992).

Stephen Perrine, ed., "Six Secrets for a Healthier, Happier, Longer Life," *Men's Health*, June 1994.

Georgia Witkin, *The Male Stress Syndrome* (New York: Newmarket Press, 1986).

Paolo Procacci, "Chronobiological Studies on Pain Threshold," *Pain* 55:2 (Nov. 1993): 277.

Stefan Lautenbacher and Friedrich Strian, "Sex Differences in Pain and Thermal Sensitivity: The Role of Body Size," *Perception and Psychophysics* 50:2 (Aug. 1991): 179–83.

Victor Parachin, "Facts of Life: A Dozen Ways to Live Longer and Better," *American Fitness*, Jan. 1994.

Don Kirkman, "Study: Women Feel More Pain Than Men," *Rocky Mountain News*, Aug. 24, 1994.

Edward Dolnick, "In the Longevity Game, the Score Is Females 6, Males 0," *Chicago Tribune*, Jan. 31, 1993.

U.S. Navy Personnel Research and Development Center, Women and Multicultural Research Office, "Effects of Sex, Marital Status and Parental Status on Absenteeism Among Enlisted Personnel," *Military Psychology* 6:2 (1994): 95–108.

EDK Forecast, "Who's Plagued by PMS?," *USA Today*, undated.

Cathy Perlmutter, Toby Hanlon, and Maureen Sangiorgio, "Triumph Over Menopause," *Prevention* 46:8 (Aug. 1994): 78.

Mary Beth Crocker, "Doctor Disputes Menopause Myths," *Cincinnati Enquirer*, Nov. 27, 1994.

Betty Friedan and Jean Block, "Why Women Age Longer and Better Than Men," *Good Housekeeping*, Oct. 1993.

Daniel Goleman, "The Secret of Long Life? Be Dour and Dependable," *New York Times*, Nov. 9, 1993.

Dietary Guidelines, U.S. Department of Agriculture/U.S. Department of Health and Human Services, *Home and Garden Bulletin* 232, 3rd ed., 1990.

"Sleep in America," Gallup Poll, 1991.

Nick Gallo, "Beating Insomnia: Up-to-Date Advice to Help You Get a Good Night's Sleep," *Better Homes & Gardens* 72:12 (Dec. 1994): 78.

Sue Watkins, "Why It's the Bizzz to Sleep Alone," *Daily Mirror*, Aug. 10, 1994.

CHAPTER 10

PRODIGY Poll, Jan.–Feb. 1995; 14,070 people.

Employee Relations I.Q. Management Consultants survey, 1994; 19,000 employees.

Marcia Brodsky, "Successful Female Corporate Managers and Entrepreneurs: Similarities and Differences," *Group and Organizational Management* 18:3 (Sept. 1993): 366.

Rebekah Maupin, "Successful Supervisors Exhibit 'Androgynous' Traits," *Manage* 41:2 (Aug. 1989): 10.

Redbook Motherhood Survey, March 1992; 1,000 mothers with children.

Cable News Network/*USA Today* poll, Aug. 1993; 1,065 adults.

Sports Illustrated poll, *American Male*, Dec. 1991; 2,320 adults.

Virginia Slims American Women's Poll, May 1990; 4,000 adults.

Marla Dickerson, "Women Bosses Get High Scores," *Detroit News*, Feb. 16, 1994.

Paul J. Toomey, "Who's the Better Boss," *Bergen* [N.J.] *Record*, July 25, 1994.

Janet Kidd Stewart, "Female Bosses: An Improvement on Male Model?," *Chicago Sun-Times*, Feb. 20, 1994.

Pepper Schwartz, "Families Blessed with Stress," *Dallas Morning News*, Nov. 28, 1994.

Pepper Schwartz, *Peer Marriage: How Love Between Equals Really Works* (New York: Free Press/Macmillan, 1994).

Philip Blumstein and Pepper Schwartz, *American Couples: Money, Work and Sex* (New York: Morrow, 1983).

Carol Kleiman, "Working Women Quell Child-Guilt Myth," *Orlando Sentinel Tribune*, Aug. 26, 1993.

Karen S. Peterson, "Many Women Say Their Place Is in the Home," *USA Today*, Sept. 20, 1993.

Alice H. Eagly, "Gender and the Emergence of Leaders: A Meta-Analysis," *Journal of Personal and Social Psychology* 60:5 (May 1991): 685–710.

Alice H. Eagly, "Gender and Social Influence: A Social Psychological Analysis," *American Psychologist* 38:9 (Sept. 1983): 971–81.

Alice H. Eagly and Blair T. Johnson, "Gender and Leadership Style: A Meta-Analysis," *Psychological Bulletin* 108:2 (Sept. 1990): 233–56.

Mary Nemeth, "When the Boss Is a Woman," *Maclean's*, Oct. 4, 1993.

K. Bartlett, "Sexual Harassment May Be Issue of the '80s," *Portland Oregonian*, Feb. 28, 1982.

Michael Walker, "Engendering Confidence," *News Tribune*, Jan. 12, 1994.

Diana Bilimoria and Sandy Kristin Piderit, "Sexism on High: Corporate Boards," *New York Times*, Feb. 5, 1995.

Diana Bilimoria and Sandy Kristin Piderit, "Board Committee Membership: Effect of Sex-Based Bias," *Academy of Management Journal* 37:6 (1994): 1453–77.

CHAPTER 11

PRODIGY Poll, Jan.–Feb. 1995; 14,070 people.

Dan P. McAdams, Renee M. Lester, Paul A. Brand, William J. McNamara, et al., "Sex and the TAT: Are Women More Intimate Than Men? Do Men Fear Intimacy?," *Journal of Personality Assessment* 52:3 (Fall 1988): 397–409.

Richard S. Cimbalo and Debora O. Novell, "Sex Differences in Romantic Love Attitudes Among College Students," *Psychological Reports* 73:1 (Aug. 1993): 15–18.

Claire J. Anderson and Caroline Fisher, "Male-Female Relationships in the Workplace: Perceived Motivations in Office Romance," *Sex Roles* 25:3–4 (Aug. 1991): 163–80.

C. Rubenstein, "The Modern Art of Courtly Love," *Psychology Today* 26:6 (July 1983): 40–49.

Martha L. Bruce and Kathleen M. Kim, "Differences in the Effects of Divorce on Major Depression in Men and Women," *American Journal of Psychiatry* 149:7 (July 1992): 914–17.

"Attitude/Relationships: Guys and Gals: Guess Who's Better at the Romance Game?," *Marketing to Women*, Feb. 1994.

Virginia Slims American Women's Poll, May 1990; 4,000 adults.

Ladies' Home Journal study, Feb. 1988; 614 married women.

David Lester, "Romantic Attitudes Toward Love in Men and Women," *Psychological Reports* 56:2 (April 1985): 662.

Mademoiselle study, 1994; 1,831 women.

Mike Tapp, "Forget Romance," *Tampa Today*, Nov. 10, 1994.

Michael Liebowitz, *The Chemistry of Love* (Boston: Little, Brown, 1983).

"Modern Love: Old-Fashioned Romance," American Floral Marketing Council survey, March 1993; 1,000 people.

"Petal Power," FTD/Roper survey, *Marketing to Women* 6:5 (Feb. 1993).

"Sex in America Today: A Comprehensive National Survey," *Parade*, Aug. 7, 1994.

"Isn't It Romantic? Survey Finds Romance Is Still Alive and Well in America," *PR Newswire*, Feb. 11, 1994.

Beth Livermore, "The Lessons of Love: Research on Falling in Love," *Psychology Today*, March 1993.

Georgia Witkin, "Infatuation," *Health*, Sept. 1984.

"Suddenly, Romance Is Hot," *Saint Tammany Times-Picayune*, Feb. 5, 1994.

"Do You Make Love?," *Redbook* survey, Roper Center, Aug. 1993; 1,000 mothers with children.

Georgia Witkin, *The Male Stress Syndrome* (New York: Newmarket Press, 1986).

Karen Peterson, "Relationships Matter," Gannett News Service, Mar. 31, 1993.

"The Keri Report: Confidence and the American Woman," Westwood Pharmaceuticals, March 1988; 1,011 people.

CHAPTER 12

PRODIGY Poll, Jan.–Feb. 1995; 14,070 people.

Women's Attitudes 1987, *Glamour* magazine poll; 800 women.

"Do You Make Love?," *Redbook* survey, Roper Center, Aug. 1993; 1,000 mothers with children.

"Poll of 500 Women Finds Many Favor Rest, Romance over Sex," Hearst Newspapers, May 16, 1994.

Samuel S. Janus, Ph.D., and Cynthia L. Janus, M.D., *The Janus Report on Sexual Behavior* (New York: John Wiley & Sons, 1993).

Jeanette Lauer and Robert Lauer, "Marriages Made to Last," *Psychology Today*, June 1985.

"Single (Never-Married) Persons as Percent of Total Population by Sex and Age," *Statistical Abstract of the United States*, 1992.

"Unmarried Couples," *Statistical Abstract of the United States*, 1993.

"Households, by Characteristic of Householder," *Statistical Abstract of the United States*, 1993.

J. Ross Eshleman, *The Family* (Needham Heights, Mass.: Allyn & Bacon, 1991).

Kris Bulcroft and Margaret O'Connor, "The Importance of Dating Relationships on the Quality of Life for Older Persons," *Family Relations* 35 (July 1986): 397–401.

Bruce Lemon, Vern Bengtson, and James Peterson, "An Exploration of the Activity Theory of Aging," *Journal of Gerontology* 27 (1972).

Douglas Kimmel, *Adulthood and Aging* (New York: John Wiley & Sons, 1990).

CHAPTER 13

PRODIGY Poll, Jan.–Feb. 1995; 14,070 people.

Virginia Slims American Women's Poll, May 1990; 4,000 adults.

"The Keri Report: Time, Nurturing and the American Woman," Bristol-Myers Squibb Company, March 1991; 1,253 people.

Bill Rumbler, "Rules for Relationships," *Chicago Sun-Times*, Feb. 14, 1993.

Sharon Waxman, "The French Mythtique," *Washington Post*, July 21, 1993.

Roper survey for Lifetime Cable Network, May 10, 1987; 991 women, eighteen to sixty-four years old.

CHAPTER 14

PRODIGY Poll, Jan.–Feb. 1995; 14,070 people.

"Age Difference Between Bride and Groom," U.S. Department of Health and Human Services, 1991.

Mary Tannen, "The Oldest Lie," *Allure*, May 1994.

Clinique Truth and Beauty Survey, Aug. 1994, Clinique Laboratories; 1,001 women.

Betty Friedan and Jean Block, "Why Women Age Longer and Better Than Men," *Good Housekeeping*, Oct. 1993.

Ann Japenga, "Face Lift City," *Health*, March–April 1991.

Georgia Witkin, "Beat the Clock," *Health*, March 1987.

Penny Ward Moser, "The New Fountain of Youth," *Self*, Sept. 1992.

Maura Rhodes Curless, "Only the Fit Stay Young," *Self*, Sept. 1992.

"The Replens Report," Parke-Davis Pharmaceuticals, June 1993; 1,014 women.